PORCELAIN

COFFEE-POT PAINTED WITH CHINESE FIGURES
By J. G. Herold. Meissen; about 1730
Munich, Bayerisches National-Museum

PORCELAIN

AS AN ART AND A MIRROR OF FASHION

BY

ROBERT SCHMIDT

DIRECTOR OF THE SCHLOSSMUSEUM BERLIN

TRANSLATED AND EDITED WITH AN INTRODUCTION BY

W. A. THORPE

ASSISTANT KEEPER IN THE VICTORIA AND ALBERT MUSEUM

With Eight Plates in Colour and Two Hundred other Illustrations

GEORGE G. HARRAP & CO. LTD.

LONDON BOMBAY SYDNEY

1932

First published 1932
by George G. Harrap & Co. Ltd.
39–41 *Parker Street, Kingsway, London, W.C.2*

PRINTED IN GREAT BRITAIN AT THE PITMAN PRESS, BATH

PREFACE

INNUMERABLE books on porcelain have appeared since the opening of the century, and it requires no little courage to undertake a new volume on the subject. The existing works, almost without exception, have approached the subject from a purely technical point of view; they are concerned only with the history of factories, painters, and modellers. An exception must be made of some of the big monographs, which do consider their special factory in its other aspects. But hitherto there has been no attempt to write a history of porcelain in its general relation to culture, even though such a study would illuminate both the history of porcelain and the history of culture.

The present volume is a first essay towards that end—and I say advisedly an essay, since the full and final treatise is still to be written. Experts who are acquainted with the various matters which I discuss will find many gaps; but they will, I hope, allow me credit for giving a neat synoptic view of widely scattered material which had been already brought together, and at great labour, by earlier workers in the history of art.

In a subject like porcelain it is obviously impossible to ignore the evolution of the art. In giving a general historical outline I have tried to describe not only the idioms of the great factories and of the great artists whom they employed, but the phases of a period style and their inevitable reaction to it.

The Golden Age of European porcelain, beginning with Augustus the Strong of Saxony and ending with Marie-Antoinette, is obviously the main theme of the present study; the later period could only be touched briefly at one or two points. Similarly the Far East—though it set the standard for Europe—has only been considered by way of introduction.

I hope that connoisseurs of porcelain will find in the following chapters a better understanding of their subject, and something worth adding to mere expertness in dates and marks, in 'right' and 'wrong.' I hope, too, that this little book will do something to make new friends for the precious substance, and for the rare and lovely art which has ennobled it.

For photographs of all objects from Mannheim collections I am indebted to the Historisches Museum, Mannheim. Thanks are due also to other museums and to private collectors who kindly supplied photographs of objects in their collections.

ROBERT SCHMIDT

FRANKFORT-ON-THE-MAIN

CONTENTS

ILLUSTRATIONS

PLATES IN COLOUR

ILLUSTRATIONS IN THE TEXT

PORCELAIN

ILLUSTRATIONS

PORCELAIN

ILLUSTRATIONS

PORCELAIN

ILLUSTRATIONS

INTRODUCTION

PORCELAIN, says Professor Schmidt, is fashion and art. In England we have always been rather shy of it; there is so much fashion that the art is obscured. The esteem of porcelain has been further damaged by the china statuettes and grand vulgarian services of the Victorian dining-room. Appreciation of its peculiar arts has thus dwindled into a fondness for old china, partly indefinite reverence for one's great-grandmother and partly recollection of an essay by Charles Lamb. It is mainly a fondness for 'old English china'; and it is an astonishing thing that arts so German, so French, so anything-but-English, should get some prestige from our sense of insularity. In England 'Dresden' has been distantly admired as courtly and Continental, and since the time of Lady Charlotte Schreiber the English factories have had their followers; it is Chelsea or Bow as it might be Chelsea or the Arsenal. There is now a new interest and a porcelain society; but as a race we have never had an instinct for porcelain, either as artists or as amateurs.

Feeling for porcelain is not the same thing as feeling for pottery, but it is the same kind of thing. The materials are so different in degree as to be different in quality. Their physics, and therefore their æsthetics, do not provide the same opportunities to an artist who handles them. Each stuff has its own niceness, is more 'agreeable,' in Coleridge's word, or less 'agreeable.' The difference in taste is elementary and physical, like a preference for natural stones. Where pottery and porcelain are alike is in the techniques which use them as media. Each of them is the material of two arts which are not always distinguished, and not the least value of Professor Schmidt's treatment is that he makes clear the distinction by the arrangement of his book.

The first art common to pottery and porcelain is ceramic, which is the art of making vessels of earthy substance by the aid of a potter's wheel. With the possible exception of glass-making ceramic is the most peculiar and isolated of artistic processes. Only certain things can be done with its wheel and its plant, and free design must submit to what *can* be done. There is the wheel, flat and fixed and rotating, and there are the free, mobile hands. In this congruence of circumstance and impulse, condition and opportunity, a pot begins. There is also the kiln. Before and after firing the pot may get some increase of appeal from glaze in colour and surface, from painting in colour and design, from other procedures which I need not detail; but the first and essential function of the kiln is to perpetuate the movement of the wheel and the hands. The wheel and the hands may give away some chances in design to ensure this permanence, for the kiln has its preferences of shape; but it is the wheel and the hands that make the primary artistic values of a pot, whether it be a pot of pottery or a pot of porcelain.

The pot is a hollow thing, and the potter uses its hollowness for the first value of his art. This is *volume*, an intentioned and rhythmic bulge. The pot has also *size*, and this too is limited by the nature of the technique. Large size is impressive, but that is not itself an artistic value, though it may be used for artistic effect. The pot, again, has a thickness of its sides, or *mass*, and since you cannot make a monument of egg-shell nor a teacup of quarter-inch earthenware, mass varies with size. It is apt to vary inversely with the amount of volume; pots are seldom thickest at the greatest bulge, because that is the point where sides tend to grow thin beneath the potter's fingers. A pot seen as flat, as a two-dimensional object, has an outline, or *profile*; and though most pots have a stance, and therefore a usual stance profile, there are infinite other profiles according to the angle of visual approach. In a good pot *any* profile is satisfactory as linear rhythm or 'drawing,' and, since it is declared by volume, it is consonant with volume. Finally, ceramic art, though it may be complete without *surface ornament*, is, I think, restricted by the lack of it. But this ornament is of a special kind. The surface which serves as a ground is not a flat panel, but a rounded surface that comes back upon itself. Good ceramic ornament not only adapts itself to volume, but serves to declare it. The design is not perceived as a flat design is perceived; it must be followed in time rather than taken in space. And while ceramic ornament must give something to the pot, it gets something in return—a surface, or ground, which contributes to its effect. When the pot is of glazed porcelain this is of great importance; good porcelain decoration does not smother the white surface, but appears on it, as was well understood by the K'ang Hsi painters, by Meissen in its early days, at Chantilly and other European factories.

Ceramic art is the orchestration of these five values—volume, size, mass, profile, and surface ornament, including glaze. Like the several techniques which in England go by the name of 'sculpture,' it is a three-dimensional art, and not to be fully enjoyed or appraised by the eye alone. Profile, colour, even texture, can be seen; to a limited extent volume can be perceived visually, just as it can be represented visually in a flat painting; but an art whose material is solid and agreeable needs the final exploration of the hand. The rhythm of volume is to be felt with the fingers, and though a pot cannot always be stroked, I think it is always seen in a hope that it may be. The desire to touch is the first test of whether a pot is a good pot; and if ceramic is less highly esteemed than painting, not the least reason is the fact that in museums and in private houses pots are almost always phantoms behind glass, with only their profile and their colour to recommend them. In England particularly art means paintings, because paintings may be seen by every one, and seen is all they can be. Sculpture and ceramic are of lower repute, because they are too well protected by DO NOT TOUCH.

The nature of ceramic is more evident in pottery, but it is not less real in porcelain. It is more evident in pottery because the primary values of a pottery pot come directly from the wheel and the hands. The stuff is crude by comparison with porcelain; it is only there to sustain form, glaze, ornament. Porcelain, on the contrary, has two qualities which attract the emphasis toward themselves, and away from the ceramic values of the wheel and the hands. The first of these is complexion. The distinguishing characteristics of porcelain, which Professor Schmidt describes, do not mean that it is a better medium than pottery, but only that it is *finer*. It is finer to handle, if it can get through the fire, but above all it is finer to look at. The early potters in porcelain were bound to use this quality of their material, and complexion began to compete with volume and profile. When complexion was used for its ground values, and with some reticence of design, it may be fairly said to have earned its place. That leads to the second quality of porcelain, its aptitude for ornament. Plastic ornament was an elaboration, and often a confusion, of profile. Painted ornament tended to turn a vessel into a vehicle. It masked volume; the white rotundity was covered too much. Perhaps the decoration which best kept the equivalence of white ground and coloured design was the type known as Kakiemon, as it was invented in Japan and copied or adapted in Europe. A similar equivalence is to be found in types of decoration which were original in Europe—some designs of *deutsche Blumen* are examples; but, on the whole, overloading of the ground has been the arch-enemy of decorated porcelain.

Although complexion and ornament compete with the primary values they do not banish them. Porcelain ceramic succeeds best when it gets all it can from the wheel and the hands, when its vessels in spite of complexion and ornament can still be considered as pots. Good potting in porcelain is not the same thing as good pottery potting, but it is good potting that makes a short list from a hundred pieces of eighteenth-century porcelain. Meissen, particularly in her early vases, succeeds because volume and profile, though dressed, are not entirely disguised—*e.g.*, Fig. 26. The Plate facing p. 124 is a magnificent example of good form carrying its limit.

The second art which may use porcelain as its medium is plastic. Plastic means modelling in a soft medium by the use of the hands and a few simple tools. This art of porcelain shares with ceramic the kiln and the exigencies of firing; it is also a three-dimensional art, but there the similarity with ceramic ends. The essential acts are different. Plastic has used clay or pottery as well as porcelain, and here, at any rate, porcelain is at no disadvantage from being too fine; the work of Kändler or Bustelli is at least as good as anything done by the modellers of T'ang times. Plastic in porcelain has shown a tendency to natural representation. There is no necessity about this, no reason why a shepherdess should be 'natural' from the flowers in her fingers to the buckles of her shoes. Simplification in porcelain is largely an unused opportunity; and a good one, provided abstraction is in terms of curve and volume rather than in terms of straight line and plane. Historically porcelain plastic has always been representational, for when porcelain was invented in Europe the humanist tradition was toward representation; the fineness of the new material encouraged it, and the tradition was reasserted in the 'ideal naturalism' of the *Klassizismus*. Thus plastic was largely modelling from life, limited on the one hand by the prevailing fashion of rococo, on the other by the kiln. Sèvres, as Professor Schmidt points out, respected the kiln and modelled compactly for safety first; Meissen, Nymphenburg, Frankenthal defied the kiln magnificently in order to be rococo.

Neither of these two arts has been really understood or assimilated in England. To appreciate either plastic or ceramic one must be a good sensualist, and as a race the English are not good sensualists. We have no sense of solids or desire to fondle them. We have little sculpture and little liking for it, nor the delicate sensuality that porcelain demands. We live by eye, and our arts are the visual arts. In pottery we have had some attainment, but even here we did our best to reduce a three-dimensional art to a flat art. The slip-ware dishes made at the end of the seventeenth century by the Toft family are perhaps the best of English native pottery, but they are flat decoration in clay. Some of the Delft wares made at Bristol are an English idiom and of excellent design, but their chief value is that of painting on an enamel surface. Even Staffordshire created few shapes, but borrowed from China or refined the antique. At the time of the *Klassizismus*, *basso-rilievo* was equally admired with 'sculpture' in the full round, and Flaxman's designs for Wedgwood were as flat and linear as in the circumstances they could be. One might expect some sympathy for horse-flesh, yet the steeds in our sporting prints have surface without body, although the Dutch painters, with their limbs and fruit, had won three dimensions from a flat canvas. Our genius for being flat was expressed in water-colour, an art deserving of higher reputation and one which may be claimed as entirely our own.

Nor had England much sympathy with the fashion which used porcelain. The style known as rococo dominated the art of Europe roughly between the years 1740 and 1780, but in this respect England was provincial to the Continent, and the vogue began here a little later than in Germany and France. For English rococo we have no better name than 'Chippendale.' Every country is apt to write the history of its own arts and to exalt provenance at the expense of period; Louis Seize, *Klassizismus*, Adam, are three names for what was in essentials the same style. Similarly rococo, as mood, fashion, art, was of Europe and without nationality. It was the same with porcelain, and Professor Schmidt makes the case very clear in tracing the migrations of workers in porcelain and the international character of their sources of design.

When European porcelain was invented humanism had gone rather dry, for the century of 'solid reason' was not long over. The times were becoming less solid and more reasonable, but the ornament of 'solid reason,' which we call baroque, still ruled Europe with a dead hand; one has only to look at the Nuremberg pattern books or the earlier designs on Rouen faience. The stir in this waste of symmetry was a Northern and romantic stir, which had already shown itself early in the seventeenth century in the paintings of Rembrandt and Van Goyen. Contacts with the Far East were affecting the mind of Europe and quickening invention in European art; but the reaction to China, as Professor Schmidt shows in one of the most interesting parts of his book, was essentially a romantic reaction. It was the Northern countries of Europe who discovered the Far East, and they created in *chinoiserie* a romantic style which contributed not a little to the making of rococo. The mood of rococo was gathering pace during the first quarter of the eighteenth century. Ten years later it had begun to show itself in design. Who is to say whether Paul Lamerie silver or 1735 Meissen is more baroque than rococo or more rococo than baroque? One cannot lay a finger on the first asymmetry or the first sentiment. By the middle of the eighteenth century the romantic mood had fully expressed itself in European art, and had created a style of greater vitality than any which had been seen in Europe since the early Renaissance.

The mood of rococo is sometimes held to be 'sophisticated,' and 'sophisticated' presumably means 'surprised at nothing.' The trouble with rococo is that it was too fond of surprises, that modern taste is too 'accustomed' to follow its innocence; the rococo artists went off into scrolls because they enjoyed it and could get a design from their enjoyment. The verdict might be a little different if rococo art had been buried for two or three thousand years; if you compare the back-piece of a group by Bustelli (*e.g.*, Fig. 137), or Lück's group in the Plate facing p. 252 with the scrolled *ensemble* of some of the Scythian bronzes which have been published by Professor Gregory Borofka,[1] the two moods are of the same kind. Rococo was the breaking of an inhibition, and a little savage in consequence.

'Sophistication' there certainly was, but only in the *fashion* of rococo. By fashion I do not mean 'influence.' Influence refers to the psychology of an artist, and implies an assimilation of one man's work by another, either by spontaneous attraction or as the result of teaching. It is uncalculated and often unconscious. Fashion, on the other hand, is a social and commercial fact; social, because it arises in a desire to be like one's fellows, but rather better; commercial, because there are profits to be made from this desire. What historians of art call a 'style' begins in mood or influence; it is sustained, developed, distributed by fashion, and if there be an artist of original power who would earn his living or represent his age,

[1] *Scythian Art* (London, Benn, 1928).

he must work within the limits that fashion imposes and with the organs of appeal that the 'style' allows him. Bustelli had to use the scroll, but he and his scroll were better than rococo.

The rococo style, in ornament (see, *e.g.*, Plates facing pp. 124, 252), in composition (*e.g.*, Fig. 200), and in expression or sentiment (*e.g.*, the left-hand figure in Fig. 133), is so well illustrated and described by Professor Schmidt that I need not refer to it in detail. What is of special interest is the mechanics of trade in rococo: books of ornament, specialist painters, specialist engravers, fashion plates, engravings after paintings, models after engravings, models after models, imitation and migration among artists, speculation and calculation by dealers, and a reception by the public which was by turns response and demand. In that sense all 'styles' are sophisticated, and we may suspect that art has gained by the sophistication. Art needs habits to save itself for its actions; and even on the lowest level of period output rococo is not more dull nor more messy than the hack-work of the Middle Ages.

Professor Schmidt has found adjectives for rococo; lively, sensitive, naughty, are perhaps the most descriptive. It is low in general esteem because its peculiarities are the peculiarities of transition. It is neither quite humanist nor quite romantic, but takes its qualities from both moods, and so mixes them that consistency is cheated. From that mixture it gets a strong character. As regards design it did not merely admit asymmetry. Asymmetry was its nature; we may give it that negative description just because it repudiated a sterile Renaissance; if it is not easy in modern Europe to agree with a style which is anti-symmetrical, that is because the heritage of 'solid reason' is still working in our minds. On the side of expression rococo was both soft and hard. In admitting sentiment it looked forward to the nineteenth century; the magazine-cover and chocolate-box style comes straight from J.-B. Greuze (1725–1805). But rococo still had the serenity of humanism, and it put sentiment in its place, allowed for it, even patronized it, with an evident detachment like the detachment of the theatre. Painters such as Boucher, Watteau, Greuze, did not hesitate to work for feeling by stress, pose, colour, facial 'registration'; half their art lies in the rendering of it. What turned having sentiment into allowing for it was the use of conventions—the convention of allegory, the convention of Italian comedy, the pastoral convention, the Chinese convention. The porcelain-modellers assumed them as an actor takes his part, so that sentiment was neither denied nor indulged, but detached and set free. It was the catharsis of the Athenian stage, evident in rococo porcelain because it was in the life of the time; and perhaps the most interesting part of Professor Schmidt's book is the section where he described the plays, ballets, masked balls, masquerades, and other means by which the eighteenth century was able to throw its feelings on to a screen and dissect them almost while they were enjoyed.

From the rococo style there emerged idioms and original art. In porcelain the idioms were mainly those of factories, rather than of nations or individuals. The factory was the productive unit, and often employed men of foreign nationality. It was the fortune of many of the ablest plastic artists to lose their identity in a collective enterprise, and we may be justified on that account in seeking among the figures of the great French and German factories the best 'sculpture' that the eighteenth century produced.

For in a very real sense porcelain *is* rococo. An age is perhaps known better by the arts which it creates than by those which it inherits, and this is particularly true of porcelain. The arts of porcelain, ceramic and plastic, were born actually into a baroque world, and Kändler and early Meissen are great names; but porcelain was not *European* as long as it was baroque. Porcelain and rococo swept Europe together; they reached their most characteristic attainment hand in hand; porcelain is the own art of the age of rococo in the same sense that stained glass is the own art of the Middle Ages.

I have written this introduction mainly for praise of the German modellers, but towards Bustelli rather than towards Kändler. It is rather a different stress from that which Professor Schmidt makes in the following pages. Kändler, by contrast with Bustelli, has a classic repose; he was a stronger modeller and perhaps a greater artist. But though he created porcelain plastic he was a creature of baroque, and porcelain, on the whole, was not a baroque art. Bustelli, on the contrary, was created by the stuff and the style; he enjoyed the paste and enjoyed rococo. He had quite forgotten that porcelain was made in a laboratory, and that some one some day would have to fire his groups for him. He was the happy modeller where Kändler was the solemn modeller, and he had, besides, a sense of decoration that Kändler never dreamed of. It is interesting to compare his larger groups with some of the Scythian bronze ornaments to which I have already referred. Theme and technique are so different that the comparison may seem a bold one, but the two arts show in one respect a common artistry; each carries the mood of the represented subject into the abstract scrolls of the *entourage*. In the Scythian bronzes the scrolls which are the unit of composition first define the subject, usually two beasts in conflict, but they do not stop at that; continued into antlers, wings, woody backgrounds, and the like, they form a decorative *nimbus* in the same emotional key as the main theme. The design may be described as 'animal line,' because you can never quite tell when it is itself animal and when it represents animals. Bustelli in his own mood and material discovered a similar effect. He set his key in the modelling of the figures, and then carried it into the base and back-piece which supported them, so that figures and *entourage* formed a single composition. He got into his abstract scroll-work the 'expression' of his figures, and composed his figures in the same rhythm as his scrolls. As an artist Bustelli perhaps gains more by his genius for expressive ornament than he loses by Kändler's power in modelling and range of interest. The Bustelli scroll is, I think, the simplest and most exciting motive in the whole of rococo ornament.

We know almost everything of Kändler. Of Bustelli we know little but his name and his works, and in this fact we may perhaps see a certain significance. Behind his art there was a whole civilization. In flesh of porcelain he was the mind of rococo and the soul of the stage which he represented. He seems to model not with his hands only, but with his whole body; he had an actor's joy in positions and an actor's flexibility of mood and limb. He became in an instant the figure he was modelling: Turk or Chinaman, cavalier or lady, swaying the crinoline, kissing the fingers, concluding arch smile or inviting glance in the sweeping mockery of a white scroll. But his figures are more than picturesque habit or actors' poses. Bustelli, with the ardour of Italy, had the coolness of the comic spirit. His expression of it in his porcelain figures has an imperceptible shrinkage which makes them memorable. His models are no longer puppets in porcelain, but the unnumbered laughter of man's derision of man.

Bustelli, as the climax of European porcelain, is not very well known in England, and the present book would have been worth writing and worth publishing in England if only as a background for Bustelli's art. The author, Professor Robert Schmidt, was formerly at Frankfort-on-the-Main, and is now Director of the Schlossmuseum at Berlin. He is perhaps best known in this country for his writings on glass. The present book was first published at Munich in 1925 under the title *Das Porzellan als Kunstwerk und Kulturspiegel.* Every country is bound to write its own art history, and Professor Schmidt has therefore dealt at greatest length with the German factories, particularly Meissen (Dresden). This gives an inevitable bias to his book, but a bias which critical opinion would probably accept as true in history. If any one is to write a general book on porcelain it should be a German, since the Germans invented European porcelain and have a genius for it.

In an English edition the question of English porcelain was bound to arise. In the German edition Professor Schmidt, apart from notices of Chelsea toys, devoted only one paragraph to the English factories. This may well represent the comparative value of English porcelain beside German and French, but in an English edition rather fuller treatment seemed called for, if only on patriotic grounds. I have therefore added a section on the English factories, but without upsetting the balance of Professor Schmidt's book it has only been possible to discuss them very briefly. Corresponding illustrations have also been added of characteristic English types. In preparing the English section I have been aided by the published works of Jewitt and of my colleagues Mr Bernard Rackham and Mr W. B. Honey, particularly by Mr Honey's illuminating chart of the technical traditions in England.[1] I would acknowledge gratefully a remark of Mr Rackham's which first interested me in rococo, that "the scrolls stop being symmetrical." In the text a few minor alterations have been made in the way of allusions and modes of expression more familiar to English readers; otherwise the edition of 1925 has been translated as it stands. A note on books and an index have been added.

W. A. THORPE

[1] *Old English Porcelain* (London, Bell, 1928), p. 278.

PORCELAIN

CHAPTER I

FAR EASTERN PORCELAIN

1. China

Porcelain had its origin in China. Even before the Christian era that country is remarkable for her pottery manufactures, and in the great figures of Lohans, or apostles of the Buddha, which still survive from about A.D. 1000, she has left us a series of ceramic masterpieces, astonishing in technical skill and artistic power, and without rival in later times. We do not know when porcelain was first made there, but one thing is certain, that it was not suddenly invented, as it was subsequently invented in Europe, by the patient researches of a chemical genius. It was evolved, on the contrary, by the labour of centuries, and in the course of that gradual development of the ceramic body which transformed the rude pottery of the Han dynasty (206 B.C.–A.D. 220) into the delicate stoneware of Sung times (A.D. 960–1279). Ware of a porcellanous character is found occasionally during the T'ang dynasty (A.D. 618–906), and as early as the Sung dynasty certain specimens can be described, with some assurance, as porcelain. Such are the species known as *Ting yao* and *Lung Ch'üan yao*. *Ting yao* takes its name from the kilns of Ting Chou, founded at the beginning of the twelfth century near Ching-tê Chên, subsequently the centre of the Chinese porcelain industry; it has a hard, fine, more or less translucent body and a white or yellow glaze, with impressed or delicately incised ornament in some of the finer pieces. The *Lung Ch'üan yao* (*yao* means properly 'kiln,' then 'fired,' and finally 'pottery-ware') takes its name from the Lung Ch'üan district, Chekiang. It is made of a hard, resonant, grey-white body, very like porcelain in quality and appearance, and it has a wonderful white, luscious glaze varying in colour from pale grey-green to a glossy blue-green. Whereas the Ting wares are fine and fragile and, with very few exceptions, are known only from recent tomb finds, the Lung Ch'üan wares, on the other hand, having thicker sides, were almost indestructible,

FIG. I. CELADON BOWL IN GERMAN SILVER-GILT MOUNTS
Chinese; fourteenth to fifteenth centuries. See p. 30.
Kassel, Landesmuseum

and have thus survived in comparatively large numbers. From the time of the Sung dynasty there was a considerable export trade to the Near East and Egypt, and even at this early period some pieces made their way to Europe. An example of these is the plain bowl in Fig. 1, which, about 1435, the Duke of Catzenelnbogen distinguished as something very precious by having it beautifully mounted in silver-gilt; for centuries it was in the possession of the ducal family of

Hesse, and is now an envied possession of the Landesmuseum at Kassel. The term celadon porcelain is a convenient substitute for the awkward Chinese name for these green-glazed wares. The shepherd Céladon was the hero of a novel, Honoré

FIG. 2. BOWL, TING WARE
Chinese; Sung dynasty (960–1279)
Berlin, Edgar Worch Collection

d'Urfé's *L'Astrée*, published in Paris in 1610. He always wore a cloak of a pale green shade which was then fashionable, and thus the name of the hero was transferred to the bowls and dishes with pale green glaze which were already coming to Paris in large numbers. A large jar of the contemporary Ming dynasty, with flowering stems in high relief, is illustrated in Fig. 3.

The final transition from porcellanous stoneware to true

porcelain probably dates from the short Yüan dynasty (A.D. 1279–1368), when China was under the Mongol rule. It was no doubt at this time that Ching-tê Chên, already mentioned, reached a position of importance. Ching-tê Chên lies in the north of the province of Kiangsi, and already had a long tradition of pottery-manufacture. In its immediate neighbourhood it had abundant supplies of kaolin, the essential ingredient of true porcelain, and as early as the

FIG. 3. CELADON JAR
Chinese; early Ming period (1368–1644). See p. 31.
Frankfort-on-the-Main, Kunstgewerbemuseum

Sung dynasty it saw the flames of three hundred pottery kilns, most of which were already occupied exclusively in supplying the imperial palace. Stoneware, which had hitherto been made in astonishing variety, was now superseded more and more by porcelain. The chief excellence of these stonewares lay almost always in rich, and usually monochrome, glazes of extremely delicate hue; but with the perfection of true porcelain there appeared a new principle of decoration—the painting of the ornament on the white surface of the porcelain, both under the glaze and in a variety of enamel (overglaze) colours. Porcelain treated in the new style was being made under the first Ming Emperor, Hung Wu

(A.D. 1368–98), and from these early *incunabula* the technique of painted decoration steadily developed till we come to the final masterpieces of the seventeenth and eighteenth centuries. Naturally the evolution of style did not keep pace with the development in technique; it followed inevitably the general decline of Chinese art from the monumental strength of the early period to the elegant, but completely enervated and degraded productions of the decline.

Something, therefore, must be said of technique, since some knowledge of it, however elementary, is necessary to any appreciation of the art. It must be made clear at the outset that there was a considerable difference between Chinese porcelain and the European porcelain invented by Böttger, and that this difference in the materials made a great difference in the artistic treatment of them. Porcelain consists of white kaolinic clay, the kind of clay which can be fired hardest without fusing, with the addition of a certain percentage of fusible felspar and a special preparation of quartz. When this mixture has been fired at a high temperature it becomes a perfectly close, hard, pure white, translucent mass. The glaze is similarly compounded, and is completely assimilated to the body during firing. These peculiar qualities make porcelain, from a technical point of view, superior to all other ceramic substances. Stoneware is equally hard, but it lacks the fine plastic quality and the pure white colour of porcelain. Faience is more brittle; it consists of a soft, porous, earthen body covered with a white tin-enamel to make it proof against water and to serve as the ground for painted decoration. The body of stoneware is harder and whiter than the body of faience, but its transparent glaze is softer and more frangible than that of porcelain. The difference, already mentioned, between Chinese and European porcelain is that the Chinese potter uses a smaller proportion of kaolin. In consequence the fluxing material is more effective, the temperature of the fire lower, and the resulting porcelain softer. The calciferous glaze is much more transparent, and usually shows a faintly greenish tinge. The harder European porcelain, with its greater kaolin content and its clear white glaze, is perhaps superior in many ways to the Chinese. On the other hand, the greater fusibility of Chinese porcelain is an advantage artistically, since it makes possible a glossier tone in underglaze painting, and allows a wider range of overglaze colours and a richer technical variety. Lastly we may refer to the differences in the application of the glaze. When the vessel has been shaped the Chinese potter simply lets it dry in the air, and applies the glaze by evenly repeated blasts of the thin glazing mixture, for which purpose he uses a stick of bamboo closed at one end with a piece of silk. In Europe the shaped vessel is exposed to a light fire, and then glazed by being dipped into the glazing mixture.

Only one underglaze colour is known to European porcelain —blue obtained from oxide of cobalt. All other colours have to be painted on the glaze after it has been fired. The colouring oxides are fired on the glaze by means of a fluxing material in a low-temperature muffle-kiln, and stand out on the surface in very low relief. Finally gilding is fired on in a light, but larger fire, and is then burnished by polishing. As against these few modes of decoration the Chinese potter has an abundance of technical processes for decorating his porcelain in colours. He understands coloured glazes in every shade of red, green, blue, brown, and black; these are applied to the air-dried vessel and 'come out' in a special high-temperature kiln. Other glazes (turkish blue, green, yellow, and violet-brown shades) are applied to the vessel after it has been exposed to the strong fire, and are fired on in a furnace of middling strength. These *émails sur biscuit*, being lead glazes, are translucent, and reveal the white biscuit surface of the body. By this process of enamelling on the biscuit a vessel or a figure may be glazed in monochrome, or the enamels may be used for pictorial ornament. In this the various colours are laid on side by side, bounded by contours in relief (as in *cloisonné* enamel on metal). Or, again, the enamel colours may be laid on the smooth surface direct, the outlines and details being painted in subsequently—mostly in manganese brown. This is especially the technique of porcelains of the *famille noire*, where a glossy black ground dominates the design; such

FIG. 4. PORCELAIN PAINTED IN UNDERGLAZE BLUE, WITH EUROPEAN SILVER MOUNTS
Chinese; fifteenth to sixteenth centuries
Frankfort-on-the-Main, private collection

are among the most highly priced collectors' pieces. Apart from the iron red and a black colour, which lie almost flat on the glaze, the overglaze colours of the Chinese potter, being mixed with coloured glass, stand out in marked relief, and have a glossy surface never attained by overglaze painting in

FIG. 5. VASE WITH DECORATION ENAMELLED ON THE BISCUIT (ÉMAIL SUR BISCUIT)
Chinese; about 1500. See p. 34.
Berlin, E. Baerwald Collection

Europe. Lastly the Chinese porcelain-painter had recourse to two underglaze, or high-fired, colours—blue and red. Underglaze red, procured from oxide of copper and never mastered by European potters of the eighteenth century, was a very difficult colour to manage, having a tendency to go slightly black during the firing. On the other hand, underglaze blue, procured from oxide of cobalt, attained in China

FIG. 6. VASES WITH 'FIVE-COLOUR' DECORATION
Centre, period of Chia Ching (1522–66); *right and left*, period of Wan Li (1573–1619)
See pp. 40, 41.

the greatest beauty and perfection. Like underglaze red, it was painted on the unfired, air-dried body, and then the glaze was put on and the whole vessel exposed to a strong fire (*grand feu*). This underglaze painting requires an unerring hand, since every stroke is painted on the absorbent body and cannot afterwards be altered; corrections are impossible.

These few remarks on technique must suffice here. Discussion of the artistic evolution of Chinese porcelain must be equally brief, and must be confined to essential points.

The Chinese people have a reputation for conservatism, even in the arts, but they have also a genius for pottery; and it is clear that in the course of five centuries they must have shown a marked development of style in the shaping and decoration of their porcelain. Until the Sung dynasty in China we have been concerned with particular workshops. Now begins the real mass-production of porcelain, especially in the ancient pottery town of Ching-tê Chên. By the year 1720 the population of the city had increased to nearly a million persons, most of whom made their living in the porcelain industry. Private enterprises existed at Ching-tê Chên, as in other parts of China, but all of them acknowledged the leadership and followed the style of the imperial factories, which were occupied almost exclusively in supplying the enormous demands of the Emperor's palace. In the year 1554, for example, more than 93,000 separate objects were made at Ching-tê Chên for the imperial household. The organization of the imperial factories was worked out in amazing detail. The processes of manufacture were so highly specialized that a single piece often passed through seventy hands before it was finished. In the eighteenth century there were special painters who only drew in the outlines, while others specialized in birds or flowers, figures or ornament. Thus it is scarcely surprising that the average wares show a certain conventionality of style. On the other hand, we may well be astonished at the perfection which this art attained. It was founded on tradition, and on infinite patience in the discovery of new methods. Its creations were

FIG. 7. TWO WINE-CUPS AND A FIGURE OF KUAN TI, THE GOD OF WAR

Enamel on the biscuit. Chinese; about 1700. See p. 42.

Frankfort-on-the-Main, K. Bacher Collection

works of superb taste, harmonious in form, delicate in drawing, and unrivalled in beauty of colour.

The early Ming period, from the fourteenth to the sixteenth century, is conspicuous for a certain lack of technical precision, but this defect was reduced during the following period, and quite disappeared under the great Manchu Emperor K'ang Hsi (A.D. 1662–1722). The main thing was always to restrict the craze for underglaze blue, which was then obtained from the Near East and was known as Mohammedan blue. The indigenous cobalt blue of China was first brought to perfection during the K'ang Hsi period, and this gave the painting in blue a luminous quality and a fine gradation of tone which China had never attained before, and which European porcelain of the eighteenth century never attained at all.

Although the technique of the early Ming period did not go very far, its artistic power was correspondingly greater, both in form and in painted decoration. Vessel shapes have a certain severity, an extraordinary repose, a clarity of profile which were bound to be lost in the greater fluency and neo-classical elegance of later apologues. In the early blue-painting the outlines and details were finely or boldly painted according to the character of the decoration; they were executed by broad brush-strokes in different shades of the colour (Fig. 4). A good example of enamelling on the biscuit, mentioned above, with outlines in relief is shown in Fig. 5. A brocaded pattern and figures in green, yellow, turkish blue, and light salmon colour appear on a ground of aubergine brown. In the three vessels in Fig. 6, dating from the middle of the sixteenth century and the beginning of the seventeenth, painting in underglaze blue is combined with various enamel colours. The baluster-shaped vase in the middle is decorated in green, yellow, and iron red as well as in blue, and is painted with cranes (a symbol of long life), flowers, and lucky emblems. It bears the mark of the Emperor Chia Ching (1522–66). The vase on the left, which has been cut down at top and bottom, is painted in the same colours, the decoration consisting of vases of flowers and panels of cloud-scrolls con-

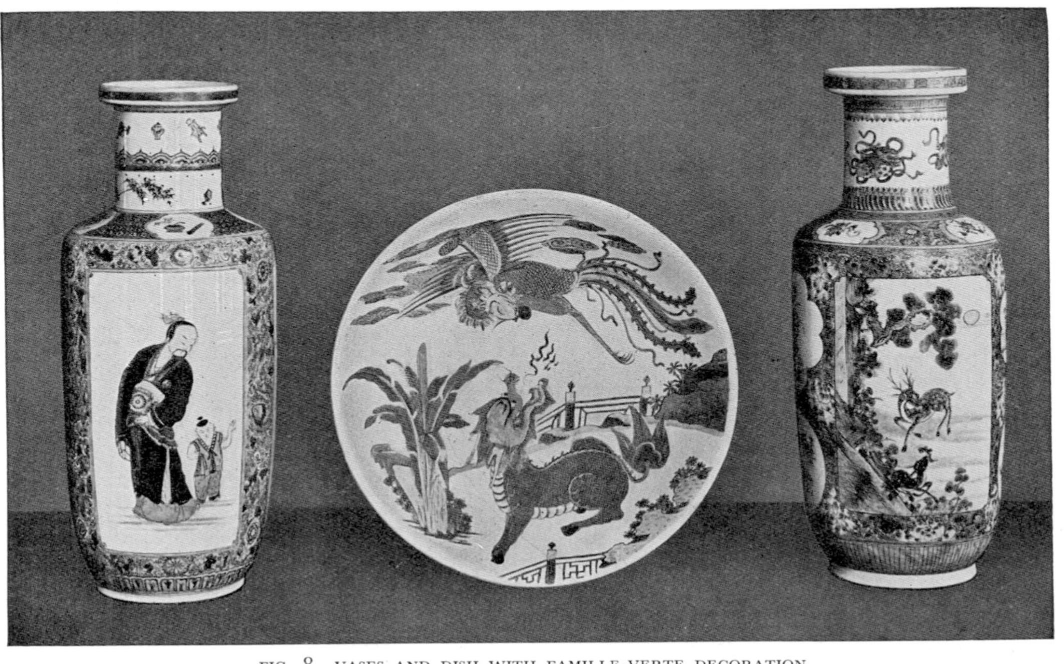

FIG. 8. VASES AND DISH WITH FAMILLE-VERTE DECORATION
Chinese; about 1700. See p. 42.
Frankfort-on-the-Main, Kunstgewerbemuseum

taining the five-clawed dragon and the phœnix, the heraldic emblems of the Emperor and Empress. The piece belongs to the period of the Emperor Wan Li (1573–1619); his reign-mark appears on the narrow-necked bottle on the right. Also of Ming date is the seated figure of the god of war (Fig. 7), Kuan Ti, a very popular subject in Chinese pottery. Here again the technique is that of enamel on the biscuit, in this case in green, yellow, and aubergine (the dark violet hue of the aubergine fruit), with the addition of a glossy black. In the same illustration the wine-cup in the form of a bull's head shows similar technical treatment, but belongs to the period of the Emperor K'ang Hsi (about 1700), under whom the art of Chinese porcelain attained its zenith. All technical difficulties had now entirely disappeared; the body was wonderfully clear, the glaze was absolutely transparent, with a surface like a mirror, while the colours had an unsurpassed brilliance. The classic shapes of Chinese vases now assumed a final elegance and distinction, and the painted decoration displayed infinite resource and incredible precision of line. All the technical discoveries of the Ming period were used and improved with an easy mastery. Underglaze blue, enamel on the biscuit, overglaze decoration in enamel colours—all reached the highest degree of efficiency and elegance. About the year 1700 the potters were specially concerned with the revival of monochrome glazes, of which the so-called *sang de bœuf*, a blood-red glaze of wonderful depth, is perhaps the most famous. In overglaze painting another triumph was a splendid glossy green derived from metal; it dominated the colour harmonies of overglaze painting, and gave the name of *famille verte* to porcelains decorated in this manner.

Under K'ang Hsi Chinese porcelain reached its zenith as a means of artistic expression, and now made ready for a rapid decline. During the following period ideas of colour changed considerably, largely owing to the growing influence of Europe. The depth and power of K'ang Hsi painting declined under the succeeding monarch, Yung Chêng (1723–35), and made way for softer between-shades, among which a lovely rose or rose red took the lead. The Chinese described this new taste

FIG. 9. VASE WITH FAMILLE-ROSE DECORATION
Chinese; about 1730
Stuttgart, Schlossmuseum

in colour as 'painting in foreign colours,' which clearly shows that they were becoming dependent on European ideas of decoration. We call these porcelains the *famille rose*, in contrast to the different palette of the *famille verte*. The characteristic rose tint, procured from gold, had first appeared in the latter part of the K'ang Hsi period, but it did not become a definite fashion in colour until the reign of Yung Chêng; its colours differed from those of the *famille verte* in that the enamels were no longer translucent, but rendered opaque by an admixture of stanniferous white. The drawing at this period took on astonishing delicacy and finesse; often it seems latent among the covering enamels, like the fragrance of a flower. Another type which had been considerably made at Ching-tê Chên, but was for the most part the speciality of Tê-hua, in the province of Fukien, is the so-called *blanc de Chine*, an undecorated porcelain of white or ivory colour with a thick, soft, velvet glaze over a soft, translucent body. In Ming times, but especially during the eighteenth century, this beautiful material was used for making fine sacrificial cups and bowls and other useful wares, but the most popular were representational works—incense-holders in the form of Buddhist lions, figures of deities such as Kuan Yin, the goddess of compassion, and Kuan Ti, the god of war, and, finally, figures and groups of Dutchmen and other Europeans in a more or less travestied version of their native costume.

FIG. 10. GROUP OF EUROPEAN FIGURES
Porcelain *blanc de Chine*. Chinese; about 1700
Kassel, Landesmuseum

The reign of the Emperor Ch'ien Lung (1736–95) brought about no further improvements. Originality and artistic power waned; the shapes lost their elegance and austerity, the painting its vigour and freshness. Technique, on the other hand, became much more accomplished. At this period there was not a subject which the Chinese painter would not have copied to the life. He took to making slavish imitations of European drawings and engravings, for which he obtained orders mostly through the East India companies. A great many vessels, with European heraldry, mythological subjects (not intelligible), Bible stories, *genre* scenes, were now produced for the European market, and at the same time special shapes and motives were used for the Siamese and Persian markets. In view of the conservative character of the Chinese it is not surprising that, side by side with these, they produced costly wares which copied, and brilliantly reproduced, the masterpieces of the Ming and K'ang Hsi periods. But the decline of the art still continued. In the succeeding reigns of Chia Ch'ing (1796–1820) and Tao Kuang (1821–50) much good work was done that was technically impeccable; but the art of porcelain had lost for ever its old glory, and in 1855 there would have been no need of the destruction of Ching-tê Chên to mark its ruin.

In the whole range of ceramic studies there is no department more difficult than that of Chinese porcelain. Apart from the very clever imitations of recent times, the masterpieces of the past were being copied as early as the fifteenth century, but especially during the eighteenth century, in response to the eclectic taste of the times. There was no question of deliberate fraud, but rather of the almost religious veneration in which the Chinese hold all the works of antiquity. Imitation even went so far as the accurate reproduction of old marks on new copies. Thus in the study of Chinese porcelain the criterion is always the style of the piece, not the mark; and it follows that the correct classification of a piece of Chinese porcelain is possible only after prolonged and exhaustive study, when one is thoroughly familiar with all the technical and artistic peculiarities of the various epochs. Even then there are quite enough uncertainties. I cannot end this section better than by quoting the warning of a book written in 1696 by a Jesuit Father, Louis de Comte, who had lived many years in China. I have already used it as the epigraph of my book *Chinesische Keramik:* "Les connoisseurs ne conviennent pas toujours dans le jugement qu'ils en portent [*sc.*, sur la porcelaine], et je vois qu'à la Chine aussi bien qu'en France l'imagination y a beaucoup de part."

2. Japan

In pottery, as in nearly all branches of useful art, the Japanese have been the ready pupils of their Western neigh-

FIG. 11. IMARI PORCELAIN
Japanese (Arita); about 1700
Dresden, Porzellansammlung

bours and cultural superiors the Chinese and Koreans. Nevertheless porcelain was not nearly so important in Japan as it was in China. Stoneware, remarkable for its glazes, held absolute sway in the Japanese pottery world. Porcelain in Japan was first made at the beginning of the seventeenth century at several places where a suitable clay had been discovered. Apart from imitations of early Chinese porcelain, amazingly clever, but lacking originality, several pottery towns in Japan have developed a style of their own. Among these Arita, in the province of Hizēn, holds first place. The products of this city are known as Imari porcelain, from the name of the seaport whence they were shipped to foreign parts. Owing to the influence of the Dutch, enormous quantities of this porcelain were exported to Europe, where they were greatly admired for their extremely delicate painting. We shall see that these wares served as models for the earliest European attempts to imitate Far Eastern porcelain. Their decoration is sensitive and graceful, and gives the white ground, with its light milky glaze, its full share in the total effect. Several beautiful shrubs, such as bamboo and prunus, and occasionally figure subjects, are painted with the greatest decorative precision in enamel colours such as green, yellow, and blue, as well as in iron red and gold. Besides these, large vases and dishes were produced—only for European export and certainly to European orders—and were decorated with lavish, but often overdone magnificence in a three-colour scheme of underglaze blue, iron red, and gold. It is interesting to note that this heavier type of Imari porcelain was also copied in China—for European export. The largest collection of Imari porcelain in Europe is in the Johanneum at Dresden.

Besides Arita, mention may be made of Kutāni, in the province of Kāga. Its material was of poorer quality, but it developed a distinctive style of decoration, consisting of yellow and purple dominated by green. In another Kutāni type red, gold, and silver were added. But Japan, as we have said, fell a long way behind the infinite variety of process and painting in Chinese porcelain; her importance in ceramic history lies solely in the great influence she exercised on the early manufacture of porcelain in Europe.

3. Export to Europe: The Chinese Style: Porcelain Rooms

We have already referred several times to the export of Far Eastern porcelain to Europe. Direct commerce between China and the countries of the Near East can be shown to have existed even before the Christian era. In T'ang times the exchange of pottery is proved by the style of certain

Chinese pottery wares and by the discovery of Chinese pottery in the West—for example, at Samarra, in Mesopotamia. Intercourse between China and Europe throughout the Middle Ages naturally occurred through the peoples of the Near East. Goods were carried to the West either by the great caravan routes through Central Asia or by the sea route round India and up the Red Sea. The Crusaders may have brought home stray pieces of this strange and costly porcelain, but, in any case, the great trading cities of Italy, Venice and Genoa, were anxious to open up trade routes from the seaports of Asia Minor and Egypt to the West.

We have already mentioned the Duke of Catzenelnbogen's celadon bowl; we may add to it three other early pieces of Chinese porcelain which can be definitely traced in Europe. The most famous is the so-called Warham Cup, bequeathed to New College, Oxford, by Bishop Warham between 1502 and 1532, and still in the possession of the college. This is likewise a plain celadon bowl, but its magnificent silver mounts again bear witness to the high esteem which Europe at that time accorded to these masterpieces of ceramic art. A pair of blue-and-white bowls with Renaissance silver mounts were brought to Weymouth in 1506 by Philip of Austria, King of Castile, and were given by him to his host, Sir Thomas Trenchard, of Wolferton Castle, Dorset. They are almost certainly an earlier document than the Warham bowl.

Blue-and-white porcelain must have reached Italy rather more frequently at the beginning of the sixteenth century, since certain specimens of Italian maioliça, particularly those of Venetian origin, dating from about 1520, are painted with motives which prove their derivation from Chinese prototypes. The Italians called this decoration *alla porcellana*. The name 'porcelain' is likewise of Italian origin, being derived from a smooth white sea creature called *porcella* ('little pig'), whose shell has some resemblance to porcelain.

Until this time, however, the importation of Chinese porcelain into Europe was an infrequent accident. The change first came in the latter part of the sixteenth century, and continued as European merchants established direct trade relations with China. After the opening up of the sea route to China the first European vessel landed on Chinese shores in the year 1517, but half a century elapsed before the

FIG. 12. PORCELAIN GALLERY IN THE MUNICH RESIDENZ
See p. 54.

Portuguese founded their first warehouse at Macao, near Canton, in 1567. In 1604 they were followed by the Dutch, and in the course of the seventeenth century the French, English, and Swedes further established their own connexions in the Far East. Everywhere East India companies were founded, and with the support of missionaries and diplomats they started a brisk trade with Chinese seaports, and began to bring whole shiploads of porcelain to Europe. They did not always succeed in getting the best wares turned out by the Chinese porcelain factories. A large part of this trade was simply export ware, mass-produced for the uncultivated tastes of foreign 'barbarians,' but owing to its beautiful material it made a great impression on Europeans, since they could not themselves produce the hard, white, resonant body of Chinese porcelain. The faience-manufacturers, who made a business of copying Ming blue-and-white, first at Delft and then in numerous German towns, could not supply the demand in sufficient quantity, at any rate so far as table wares and drinking-vessels were concerned. The fact that porcelain is a very bad conductor of heat made it extremely serviceable for warm drinks; even in the seventeenth century chocolate, tea, and coffee were being introduced, as every one knows, into the civilized countries of Europe, and rapidly became the fashionable drinks of Society. Chocolate was known in France even before the reign of Louis XIV, and was called *le lait des vieillards*, and in 1657 London acquired her first chocolate-house. Tea became known in Germany about the same time, and in 1670 coffee as well; both drinks had been introduced into France and England some time before. The larger towns almost all started coffee-houses, of which the great French *Encyclopédie* said: "Ils sont aussi des manufactures d'esprit, tant bonnes que mauvaises." But these drinks paid a heavy duty, and for a long time the enjoyment of them was confined to the upper and well-to-do classes. It is not surprising that these new and exotic drinks made the use of Chinese porcelain cups indispensable to a well-appointed household.

But the effects were quite general. Increasing familiarity with China made a profound impression on Europe, especially on European art, and resulted in a perfect mania for the Far East. In the last quarter of the thirteenth century the Venetian traveller Marco Polo had spent seven years at the palace of Kublai Khan, the Mongol Emperor of China, but the first news of his experiences had had little effect in Europe,

FIG. 13. MIRROR GALLERY IN THE MUNICH RESIDENZ
See p. 54.

being treated for the most part as a traveller's tale. Authentic accounts of this Empire of the Interior did not really find their way to the West again until members of the various East India companies and other explorers introduced European readers to the ancient civilizations of the East by descriptions of the country and its people, and especially by the engravings with which these travel books were illustrated. Books of this kind were published mainly by Dutch travellers. The earliest and most important was a great work by Johann Neuhof on a Dutch diplomatic mission to China, of which further editions appeared in various languages from 1665. There followed the works of Dr O. Dapper (Amsterdam, 1670) and S. de Vries (Utrecht, 1682). As documents the illustrations of all these works are by no means free from objection; at most they provided travellers' sketches as a basis for subsequent elaboration by European engravers. The pictures naturally contain much that is not Chinese, a certain liveliness of fancy making the treatment of the subjects an extraordinary blend of Oriental and European. This strange world excited tremendous interest in Europe, and from the end of the seventeenth century we can detect, in nearly all branches of architecture and decorative art, a great wave of Oriental influences, which gathered volume as the eighteenth century advanced, until it was superseded about 1760 by the new fashion for classical antiquity. But it never quite died out. There was a recrudescence during the *Biedermeier*[1] period.

About 1900 we found ourselves in another period still, and at the present day *chinoiserie* again holds an admittedly important place in pottery, lacquer, wood-engraving, and other arts.

Towards the end of the seventeenth century the influx of Chinese porcelain was at its height. The Oriental, or 'Indian,' fashion, as it was called, turned the heads of civilized Europe, and it is not surprising that the enthusiasm of noble collectors fastened on Chinese porcelain. In the latter part of the reign of Louis XIV and during the Regency[2] a porcelain room was indispensable to a gentleman's house, and in all the

[1] *Biedermeier* means literally 'honest yeoman.' The term *Biedermeierzeit* (*Biedermeier* period) is commonly used in Germany in reference to the rise of the middle classes during the early part of the nineteenth century and the style of decoration associated with it. The style roughly corresponds with 'Regency' and 'Empire,' but some of its associations are more suggestive of 'Victorian.'

[2] *I.e.*, the regency of the Duke of Orleans during the minority of Louis XV.

FIG. 14. MIRROR ROOM IN THE PALACE OF ANSBACH
See p. 54.
Photo Stödtner, Berlin

better drawing-rooms and *salons* the mantelpiece was adorned with a set of blue-and-white or coloured vases. These *garnitures de cheminée*, consisting as a rule of three bellied vases with covers and two slim vases known as 'flutes,' have never been made for the Chinese taste; they were simply commissions from European merchants executed in Chinese factories for the 'barbarous' white men. Porcelain rooms and porcelain galleries were frequent at this date in Germany—for example, in the Munich Residenz and in the palaces of Ansbach, Charlottenburg, Schönbrunn, Arnstadt, to mention only the most important. Naturally a good many of them, according to the date of their construction, exhibit a style of ornament which was developed in German porcelain factories of the eighteenth century. Others again, like the sumptuous Mirror Gallery in the Munich Residenz—it is after a design by François Cuvilliés, and embellished with wood-carvings of infinite variety—are decorated entirely in Oriental porcelain, which rises above gilt console-tables round the mirrors up to the ceiling (Fig. 13). Below are vases in European bronze mounts, the latter, with their warm gold colouring and delicate rococo scroll-work, relieving the cold blue-and-white of K'ang Hsi porcelain, and at the same time making a delightfully fantastic setting for the glaze-coloured beasts, peacocks, lions, and 'Dogs of Fo.'[1] To the same period belongs the delightful Mirror Room in the palace at Ansbach. Its figure decoration was carried out partly by the local porcelain works, but mostly in the factories at Meissen and Berlin. Another and extremely interesting example is provided by a room decorated about 1725 for the Dubsky Palace, at Brünn, and now erected in the Österreichisches Museum für Kunst und Industrie, at Vienna. The entire room is decorated in the earliest Vienna porcelain; even the chandeliers and branches and the entire mantelpiece are made of porcelain, while small porcelain plaques are let into the woodwork of the panelled walls and the suite. Earlier still is the porcelain room in the palace at Charlottenburg, executed in 1703 by Eosander von

[1] 'Dog of Fo' is a Chinese name for the Chinese idea of a lion. *Fo* means the Buddha or Buddhist.

Goethe. According to tradition most of the plates, dishes, and vases exhibited there form part of a gift from the English East India Company to the first Queen of Prussia, Sophia Charlotte. The remainder have been reduced more than once in later times, chiefly during the Seven Years War, but replaced in part by Meissen and other German porcelain.

FIG. 15. PORCELAIN ROOM IN THE PALACE AT CHARLOTTENBURG

The room as arranged to-day no longer gives a clear and well-balanced picture of its original condition, as it appears in a beautiful copper-engraving by its architect, Eosander von Goethe himself (Fig. 15).

How much these porcelain rooms quickened the invention of contemporary architects can be seen from numerous designs which are to be found among the architectural series of nearly all French and German engravers. The *View of the Mirror and Porcelain Room* in the palace of Pommersfelden comes from the hand of the prolific Salomon Kleiner. The work was executed, and probably designed, by one of the best Frankish cabinet-makers, Ferdinand Plitzner. The room is panelled throughout in walnut and embellished with rich gilt wood-carvings and remarkable inlaid work, even on the floor. It was completed in 1717, and has remained almost unaltered for over two hundred years, a perfect example of Regency taste: we may observe how the Chinese vases and figures displayed on their consoles take their place in the general scheme of decoration. Here again we find Callot figures, which were very popular at that period and are still used to-day, serving as centre-pieces in the decoration of the doors. Naturally the Latin countries shared the fashion for porcelain rooms; as an example we illustrate part of the wall in the porcelain room of the royal palace at Madrid. It is decorated with vases, figures, and reliefs of Buen Retiro porcelain, but belongs entirely to the late classical period (Fig. 17).

The grandest of all visions in porcelain was the equipment of the Japanese Palace at Dresden. Unfortunately this truly princely scheme was never carried into effect. Augustus the Strong, Elector of Saxony and King of Poland, was the most artistically gifted and the most ostentatious of the German princes of his time. He brought to Dresden eminent architects, distinguished painters, talented craftsmen. We may recall the important part played by his Goldsmith-in-Ordinary, Dinglinger, in the history of the goldsmith's art in Germany. It was Augustus the Strong whose urgent wishes, in conjunction with J. F. Böttger's happy invention, led to the foundation of the first manufactory of true porcelain in Europe. Of this something will be said in a moment; here we need only mention the King's high ambitions for 'his' porcelain. His ancestors had occasionally acquired pieces of Oriental porcelain, but at an early age Augustus the Strong had been seized with a passion for collecting which had already cost him a hundred thousand thalers in the first year of his reign. Thenceforward he collected all his life, wherever he could. He had agents in Paris and Holland who made purchases on his behalf, and he acquired valuable

FIG. 16. MIRROR ROOM IN THE PALACE OF POMMERSFELDEN

See pp. 55–56.

objects from the collections of the Saxon nobility. His most famous, and infamous, bargain was the forty-eight impressive 'Dragoon' vases, for which he had to give the King of Prussia a regiment of dragoons in exchange. He knew perfectly well that his passion for porcelain was a disease, and he made a striking admission of the fact in a letter to Count Flemming, in which he says: "Ne scavez vous pas qu'il est des oranges comme des porcelaines, que ceux qui ont une fois la maladie des uns ou des autres ne trouvent jamais qu'ils en ayent assez et que plus ils en veulent avoir." His collection, numbering many thousands of pieces and consisting mainly of Chinese and Japanese wares, modern at that time, is to-day the proud possession of the Porzellansammlung in the Dresden Johanneum. It is the largest collection of Oriental porcelain, and unrivalled in extent by any other collection in the world. As the attempt to produce porcelain in Saxony had been a success, the King formed the plan of holding a great 'ideal' competition between Oriental and Saxon porcelain. The Dutch Palace in Dresden-Neustadt, built in 1715 for Count Flemming by Pöppelmann, was to be the scene of the exhibition. He bought and enlarged it, and under the new name of the Japanese Palace prepared it for the reception of Oriental wares and for the large orders which he placed with his own factory at Meissen. The whole of the ground floor was to take the Chinese and Japanese porcelain, and all the walls of the galleries and rooms were to be decorated with it right up to the ceiling, each room following a different colour scheme. The upper floor was reserved exclusively for the products of the Meissen factory, and here too each room was to have its own scheme of coloured porcelain. A great central gallery was intended for colossal animal figures and birds, as well as for large vases. The throne-room was provided with a chime, which still exists, and other things, and the chapel was to have chancel, organ-pipes, and altar, as well as plastic decoration with almost life-size figures of the Apostles, all executed in porcelain. While other kings and princes were content with a porcelain room or a porcelain gallery the Polish King wanted an entire palace for the display of this

FIG. 17. PART OF THE DECORATION OF A ROOM IN THE PALACE AT MADRID

Buen Retiro porcelain. See p. 56.

lovely material. The preparation of the large figures of men and animals involved such technical difficulties that only a small proportion of them was finished when the King died. But the work was continued; and when we learn that in 1730 the porcelain kitchen utensils in the palace were alone valued at a million thalers, and again that in 1733, when Augustus the Strong died, no less than 35,798 pieces of porcelain were supplied for the Japanese Palace, we may form some idea of the dazzling splendour of this fairy castle—if only it had been completed. But the enthusiasm of the new King waned gradually; the collection was robbed for other purposes, and in the year 1775 it was banished to the palace cellars. In the course of time much of it was disposed of, and the remainder, still, of course, an enormous quantity, was eventually housed partly in the tower of the palace, partly in the Porzellansammlung in the Johanneum. When once this collection is properly exhibited the public will realize for the first time the unrivalled technical and artistic achievement of the early days of the Meissen factory; its almost ideal expression of the will-to-form of its period; and the lavish expenditure on art and luxury by which a king magnificent, "a genius for enjoying life," sought to make his capital the most glorious of royal cities.

CHAPTER II

EUROPEAN PORCELAIN

1. Böttger's Invention and the Meissen Factory

Attempts to imitate Chinese porcelain had been made at an early period. From 1470 onwards we hear of such 'inventions' in many Italian cities—Venice, Ferrara, Pesaro, and Turin—but we may take it as certain that they were all without result. Only Florence, under the rule and with the powerful support of the Grand Duke Francis I (1574–87), succeeded in producing a ceramic ware, which goes by the name of Medici porcelain, and does in fact bear some resemblance to its Oriental original. It contains kaolin, if only in very small quantity, but its coarse yellowish body had to be covered first with a white translucent tin-enamel to provide a clear ground for blue-painting which shows a mixture of Persian, Chinese, and indigenous Italian motives. But this Medici porcelain remains an episode.

About a century later, however, new experiments in France did produce certain results; the wares made at Rouen from 1673 and at Saint-Cloud from 1695 bear some resemblance to Chinese porcelain, especially the so-called *blanc de Chine*, but they lack the kaolin which is the essential ingredient of the Chinese paste. Their body is simply a white vitreous frit-porcelain with a beautiful yellowish surface, and must be regarded as the forerunner of the soft-paste porcelain of Sèvres; but from the year 1768, following the discovery of kaolin deposits at Limoges, Sèvres began gradually to produce hard-paste porcelain.

All these experiments, however, were made with little regard for purely æsthetic values, the chief motive being practical and economic. The increasing importation of Chinese porcelain was naturally followed by an increase in the amount of money which went abroad to pay for it.

Huge sums of money were spent on satisfying the passion for collecting which had seized princes and nobles and the rich merchant class. There is a famous remark of E. W. von Tschirnhausen, who contributed much to the invention of Saxon porcelain, that "China was the bleeding-bowl of Saxony." Nothing was more natural than the wish to check the flow of money to foreign countries by producing at home, and to fill the national coffers with the profits of an export trade. The enormous business done by the faience-potters of

FIG. 18. TEAPOT OF BÖTTGER'S BROWN STONEWARE
About 1715. See p. 63.
Hamburg, Tillmann Collection

Delft and the flourishing state of the faience industry at Frankfort, Hanau, and other German towns showed what large profits were already being derived from the imitation of Chinese porcelain in the ruder fabrics of faience. How much more lucrative, it was thought, must be the manufacture of true porcelain. Moreover, since the appearance of Colbert (1619–83), Minister of Louis XIV, political theory had been augmented by a 'mercantile principle': that every nation should strive to develop its industries and realize its natural resources and other products, and so render itself independent of the foreigner. Thus the attempts at imitation became more numerous, until at last fortune smiled on a research worker of brilliant intellect and untiring method. This happened at Dresden in the year 1709. It is not necessary to recite here all the events which led up to this invention—they are already

Dish with Flower-painting and Mosaic Border en Couleur de Rose
Berlin; about 1770
Munich, Bayerisches National-Museum

known well enough, and a few brief remarks will serve to keep them in mind. Originally the inventor, Johann Friedrich Böttger, was not out for ceramic discoveries. His aim was a high one—gold. The quest of the philosopher's stone played an important part throughout the Middle Ages up to the period of the Enlightenment. The alchemist in his mysterious laboratory appealed to the *macabre* fancy of the common people as well as to the cold reason of capital cities. Waste and fraud and disappointment made no difference; people were always flirting with the goldmakers in the hope that by their efforts the secret of gold might be revealed. For many centuries alchemy passed for as serious a science as any other. And now a Berlin apothecary's apprentice—a Sunday's child and predestined for alchemy—devoted himself to like studies. As the King of Prussia wanted to use him for his own purposes, Böttger fled to Saxony. But it was out of the frying-pan into the fire. Augustus the Strong had him arrested, and kept him for long years at Dresden, and on the Königstein at Meissen, working for him, and under constant supervision. In return he placed large sums of money at his disposal, and granted all his personal wishes except his desire for freedom. It was a prison of gold. For years Böttger was occupied with his alchemical quest for gold, until other of his investigations came to the front, probably owing to the encouragement of the physicist Ehrenfried Walter von Tschirnhausen, who had been greatly impressed by his abilities and was a keen collaborator with him. The thing to do now was to examine the natural resources of Saxony, especially ores, colours, clays, with a view to using them for industrial purposes; and in the course of these investigations ceramic research gradually took the first place. As many clays as possible were systematically tested to see whether they would fuse under heat, and by strictly adhering to this method Böttger soon hit on several species of clay which, after careful mixing and testing, promised to produce satisfactory ceramic bodies. The first result was a simple faience; then followed a brown stoneware, copied from a well-known type of Chinese pottery and procured by mixing a red, fire-resisting clay with an easily fused fluxing medium. The secret of preparing porcelain now lay in the use of a non-fusible, fire-resisting clay—all other 'inventors' of porcelain came to grief simply because they had overlooked this point. Having discovered a working formula,

FIG. 19. VASE OF BÖTTGER'S PORCELAIN
About 1715
Dresden, Porzellansammlung

Böttger proceeded to apply it. He now made careful tests of the 'white earth,' and after endless difficulties he succeeded in finding the right proportion of white Colditz clay—which was nothing more than true kaolin—to mix with the right fluxing medium. The second difficulty, that of making the glaze, was solved during further experiments, so that at the end of the year 1709 he was able to unpack from his kiln the first specimens of a true, though as yet imperfect, porcelain. In January 1710 the King gave orders for the erection of a porcelain factory, started at Dresden, but transferred a few months later to its permanent home at the Albrechtsburg at

FIG. 20. DRINKING-VESSEL (HUMPEN) OF BÖTTGER'S PORCELAIN WITH MONOGRAM OF AUGUSTUS THE STRONG
Mannheim, Hermannsdorf Collection

Meissen. In these early stages there was, of course, no question of producing true porcelain in the factory; Böttger had several more years' strenuous work before he could be sure that this, his greatest invention, was out of its knickerbocker stage and could be made a paying proposition. At first the factory concentrated only on the red stoneware, with which we shall deal in a moment. Böttger himself remained in his Dresden prison, the Jungfernbastei ('the Maidens' Castle'), still under observation after four years of it. He had been bound to divulge the arcanum, the secret of the composition of the body and the glaze, but he divided it between two different people, so that there was no danger of an expert getting to know the whole formula. Böttger expressed his resignation—or was it partly pride?—in an inscription which

FIG. 21. TEAPOT WITH GILT CHINESE FIGURES
Meissen; about 1720–25
Hamburg, Tillmann Collection

he placed over the door of his laboratory: "God, our Creator, has turned a gold-maker into a potter."

The factory production of porcelain was first begun in 1713, but even then there were so many failures in the firing that success was purely a matter of luck. Three years later, in 1716, the difficulties had been so far overcome that nearly all the objects packed in the kiln were properly fired and glazed when they came out of it. Böttger had discovered at last the right ingredients for the body—the most important being the so-called Schnorrsche earth, from Aue, in Vogtland—and the right proportions for mixing them. The construction of the furnaces, which had caused him much perplexity, had also been accomplished, although the great kilns which he planned were never built during his lifetime. For the present the manufacture was confined to small articles in limited numbers. Another and very urgent problem which Böttger never quite succeeded in solving was the question of painting. The most important colour, underglaze blue procured from cobalt, defeated all his efforts, and was not successfully produced until 1720, a year after his death. On the other hand, he succeeded, again after numerous failures, in discovering various overglaze colours, some of them of the

FIG. 22. PART OF A TOILET SET WITH GREY-GREEN GROUND
Meissen; about 1730
Munich, Residenz

greatest brilliance. There was also a beautiful reddish-lustre pigment, which played an important part during the next period. Decoration in gold and silver was already conspicuous during the Böttger period.

But in spite of everything much still remained to be done, both technically and artistically, when, in the spring of 1719, the inventor died. He was a man of great gifts and intellectual resource, with all the qualities of an inventor, but he was no organizer, and he lacked the business ability for managing a factory. Large sums of money had been spent on his schemes and on the porcelain-manufacture, but up to the time of his death the enterprise had always been run at a considerable loss. Even the King, who had believed implicitly in Böttger's genius, had several times lost both his faith and his patience, as more and more grants were required of him without producing any tangible results. A sensible system of administration was now introduced, unnecessary and useless jobs were eliminated, good artists and technical assistants were engaged, larger furnaces were built; and it was not long before the manufacture became a business proposition, improving year by year, and at last realizing in full all the hopes which had been vested in it at its foundation.

With the later development of the Meissen factory we shall deal more briefly; there are already too many books to read on the subject. We may notice here the most important stages of its history, a knowledge of which is absolutely essential to a wider understanding of its artistic work.

It is not unimportant to realize how the administration of the factory developed side by side with its art. At the beginning, after Böttger's death, a commission of three was appointed. Afterwards the management was for two years in the hands of the Prime Minister, Count Hoym, and after his downfall the King took over the supervision himself from 1731 until his death. In 1733 Augustus III turned over the business to his Cabinet Minister Count Brühl, who had previously taken the greatest interest in the manufacture, and together with Augustus the Strong himself had a decisive influence on both its economic and its artistic history. He held the post of director until 1763. In the following year a school of art was founded at Meissen "to succour the decline of the painting and modelling at the factory." C. W. E. Dietrich, Court painter and professor in the Academy of Arts at Dresden, was appointed principal of this institution, and the whole of the art side was placed under his control. It is significant that at this time modellers and painters were sent on tours of observation to Vienna, Paris, and the leading factories in the West and South of Germany. Meissen realized that artistically she was being left behind, and that a new economic life was only possible if some steps were taken to recover her artistic supremacy. But that aim Meissen never quite achieved. Sèvres and Vienna were the arbiters of taste, and not all the efforts of Count Camillo Marcolini during his forty years' directorate (1774–1814) could restore Meissen to her lost kingdom. The great days of Meissen, when European porcelain was revealing its own idiom, cover roughly the second

FIG. 23. TOILET SERVICE SAID TO HAVE BELONGED TO AUGUSTUS THE STRONG
Meissen; about 1730
Dresden, Porzellansammlung

quarter of the eighteenth century. Her prosperity was sustained and guided by two artists of genius, the painter J. G. Herold and the modeller J. J. Kändler. Herold came to Meissen in 1720 from the recently founded factory at Vienna, and under his leadership the painted decoration made such rapid progress that within a few years the factory reached the zenith of its technique and its art. The magnificent pieces of the period 1730–40 have never been surpassed even at Meissen. We shall speak of them later in other connexions. The post of plastic designer was held by Gottlob Kirchner from 1727 to 1728 and again from 1730 to 1733. In the interim it was filled by Ludwig Lücke. But in 1731 the

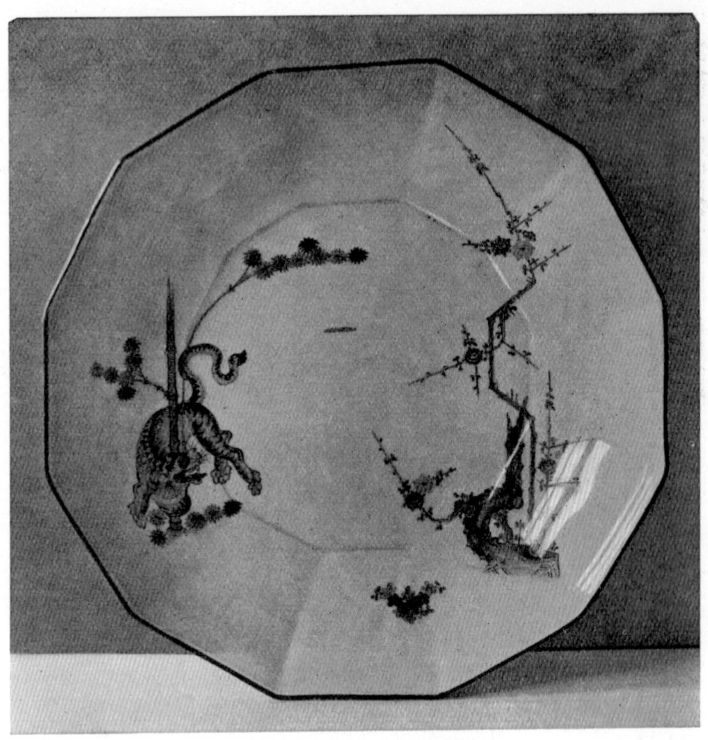

FIG 24. DISH WITH 'YELLOW TIGER' PATTERN
Meissen; about 1730
Dresden, Porzellansammlung

management had the great good fortune to engage as modeller the twenty-five-year-old sculptor Johann Joachim Kändler. After the departure of Kirchner he succeeded to the position of head modeller, and remained till 1740 under the supervision of Herold, whose activity continued until 1765. These two gifted artists, in spite of many differences and discords, worked together in a wonderful way on the creation of the great services and other problems of the factory. The purely plastic objects, including most of the figures for the Japanese Palace, of which we shall say something in a moment, the big groups, and the multitude of small figures, to us the quintessence of the art of porcelain in the eighteenth century, are Kändler's independent and most individual work. He began in the heavy, boisterous style of baroque; then, following the taste of the times, he carried the factory into rococo, readily suiting his own manner to baroque's gay and charming child. The outstanding genius of Kändler created the characteristic style of Meissen in figure-modelling, and dominated it to such an extent that lesser spirits like Johann Friedrich Eberlein (working 1735–49) are comparatively without importance for its history. From the 1760's onward the rococo style gradually gave way to the classical form of Louis Seize. The ageing Kändler could not keep pace with the perpetual transition to a new world. He was replaced by a Frenchman, Michel Victor Acier, who worked at Meissen from 1764 to 1779 and brought the new style into the ascendant. His assistants were C. Schönheit (working 1745–94), C. Gottfried Jüchtzer (1769–1812), and Johann Daniel Schöne (from 1783). But the fame of all these modellers was dimmed by the bright star of Kändler, the greatest modeller in the eighteenth-century art of porcelain and one of the greatest plastic artists that the history of statuary has ever known.

2. Other German Factories

The Meissen factory had a thorny path to travel before it fully mastered the technique and the art of so intractable a medium; but it may claim full credit for creating from nothing, entirely by its own efforts, and with no outside aid, the beautiful ceramic ware which for centuries the Western world had sought in vain, and which has become an essential of modern civilization. Naturally the invaluable secret was jealously guarded at Meissen, but without avail; the arcanum was betrayed by disloyal workmen who could not resist the persuasive manners and handsome promises of agents from abroad.

In earlier centuries the republic of Venice had imposed the death penalty on absconding glass-workers, and rigidly enforced it by assassination. The eighteenth century was more humane, and offenders were no longer exposed to these draconian measures. But even at Meissen it was several times

FIG. 25. DISH MOULDED IN RELIEF WITH AN 'OZIER' BORDER AND PAINTED WITH 'INDIAN' FLOWERS
Meissen; about 1730
Mannheim, Hermannsdorf Collection

proclaimed that deserters who were caught would be punished with imprisonment. As early as 1713 the secret of the red Böttger stoneware was carried from the Dresden laboratory to Plaue on the Havel. This competition was not dangerous; much more unpleasant was the fact that in 1717 the Austrian War Minister, du Paquier, seduced the enameller and gilder Hunger and, two years later, after Böttger's death, the foreman Stölzel from the Meissen factory, and started a porcelain factory at Vienna. As early as 1720 Hunger went on to Venice, at the invitation of the Venetian ambassador, and continued to make porcelain there till 1725. Then he repented and went off back to Meissen. Stölzel too stayed only a year at Vienna, and then he found his way back to Meissen, in the company, be it noted, of a young painter from the Vienna factory, J. G. Herold, who soon made himself, as we have said, one of the most important painters and craftsmen in the Meissen factory, brought it to the zenith of its art, and was for many years the decisive influence on its painting. The Vienna factory continued to flourish, and was soon a formidable competitor of Meissen; for the first time Meissen had lost its monopoly.

For several decades the Vienna factory had to contend with grave financial difficulties. Its founder, Claudius Innocentius du Paquier, in spite of excellent work, was already bankrupt in 1727, and in 1744 he was obliged to make over the factory to the State. Of the artists, especially the modellers, of the early period little is known. From 1747 to 1784 the distinctive style of Vienna figure-modelling was determined by the head modeller, Johann Josef Niedermayer. Thereafter the leading modeller at Vienna was Anton Grassi, an artist of considerable distinction, and probably the finest modeller in the Louis-Seize style who worked for the German factories. Financially the factory had no success until in 1784 the management was transferred to a clever and cautious merchant, Konrad Sorgenthal. He was a man of fine artistic feeling, and engaged several excellent painters as well as a notable chemist. Until 1805 he specialized in vessels decorated with sumptuous painting and elaborate gilding in the classical style, and so won for his factory the place of honour beside the products of Sèvres in the later history of the art of porcelain. Among the hitherto despised figures of the *Biedermeier* period those made at Vienna are the most worth collecting. Many of them have the poise of a work of art, and the painting is often very delicate. They are, at any rate, well above the average of the china statuettes, mostly of Thuringian origin, which have so seriously and justly discredited the porcelain made at that period. The Vienna factory ceased to exist in 1864.

It was some time before porcelain factories were actively established in German towns other than Meissen and Vienna. Meantime attempts were made to start factories in a number of cities. Some of these were quite unsuccessful, as when the 'arcanists' turned out to be impostors. In other cases success was partial; only faience was made, but it was usually described by the more attractive name 'porcelain.' When any challenge was offered to the renown of Saxony it usually came from the rulers of larger or smaller German states—temporal and spiritual lords, who had in mind, now and always, the economic interests of their several states. This 'mercantile principle' finds expression in nearly every charter of foundation where the opening clause prohibits the importation of foreign porcelain in favour of the home manufacture. Conversely, it was the constant aim to extend the market by export, by having a stall in the great fairs at Leipzig, where European porcelain from Meissen was put on the market for the first time at the Easter fair of 1713, and at Frankfort, and by establishing agencies in the larger commercial and residential cities of Germany.

After Meissen and Vienna the next German porcelain factory to appear on the map was Höchst on the Main, started in the year 1746. It was founded by a talented Meissen painter, Adam Friedrich von Löwenfinck, who had been working at intervals in various faience factories. Funds were supplied by two Frankfort business men, and a licence was granted by the Elector of Mainz. Löwenfinck moved on three years later, and his successor, Benckgraff, whom we meet again at Fürstenberg, did not stay much longer. The factory got into the usual financial straits, and in 1765 was converted into a joint-stock company in which the Elector himself had a controlling interest. Eventually it had to be worked entirely at the Elector's expense, and ceased to exist in 1796, at which date it had run the Elector into a debt of over 57,000 gulden.

FIG. 26. VASE WITH PANELS ON A YELLOW GROUND
Meissen; about 1730
Munich, Bayerisches National-Museum

Apart from Löwenfinck, the chief artists in the early days of the factory were the painter Zeschinger, who went to Fürstenberg with Benckgraff in 1753, and the modellers Simon Feilner (who accompanied them thither) and his successor Laurentius Russinger, who is known to have been at the Pfalz-Zweibrücken factory in 1767–68. The highest attainment of the Höchst manufacture is bound up with the activity of the statuary J. P. Melchior, who entered the factory in 1767, migrated to Frankenthal in 1779, and finally was working at Nymphenburg from 1797 to 1822.

The case of Höchst is a good illustration of the peculiar migrations of technicians and artists from one factory to another. The same tendency may be observed almost everywhere, and though it makes the history of German porcelain a very complicated study, it had the advantage of infusing fresh blood into the different factories.

In 1747 Höchst was followed by Nymphenburg, or Neudeck, whence the factory of the Elector of Bavaria was first transferred to Nymphenburg in 1761. It owed its earliest successes to the arcanist Joseph Ringler, of Vienna, who entered the factory in 1753 and went on to Ludwigsburg in 1759. Like Vienna, Nymphenburg used the so-called Passau earth, derived from a great bed of kaolin in the principality of Passau. The manufacture, which passed later into private hands, has had many fine achievements in the course of its history. The chief artist was the Italian Franz Anton Bustelli. His sensitive models have given Nymphenburg a high reputation for plastic work, rivalling if not exceeding that of Meissen herself. He was working there from 1754 to 1763, and was succeeded by the Bohemian Dominikus Auliczek, who again was followed by Melchior.

From 1751 the North of Germany began to compete with the West and South. At Berlin Frederick the Great granted a licence to the merchant Wegely. Wegely engaged workmen and painters from Höchst and Meissen, his modeller being the statuary Ernst Heinrich Reichard. The factory came to an end in 1757, but four years later was set going again by the merchant Gotzkowsky with the assistance of Reichard. The

FIG. 27. ENGRAVING BY J. G. HEROLD
Munich, Graphische Sammlung

new owner brought Friedrich Elias Meyer from Meissen to be head modeller and also three painters—K. W. Böhme,

FIG. 28. VASE WITH HEROLD'S CHINESE FIGURES IN PANELS ON A SEA-GREEN GROUND
Meissen; about 1730–35
Frankfort-on-the-Main, Kunstgewerbemuseum

Balthasar Borrmann, and K. J. Christian Klipfel. By 1763 the staff had increased to the considerable number of 146 persons. Gotzkowsky, however, got into financial difficulties, with the result that the King thought it necessary to buy the factory; and thereafter it was run as the royal, or, as we should say now, the national factory. Here also Passau earth was used, later on with the addition of a clay from the Schweidnitz

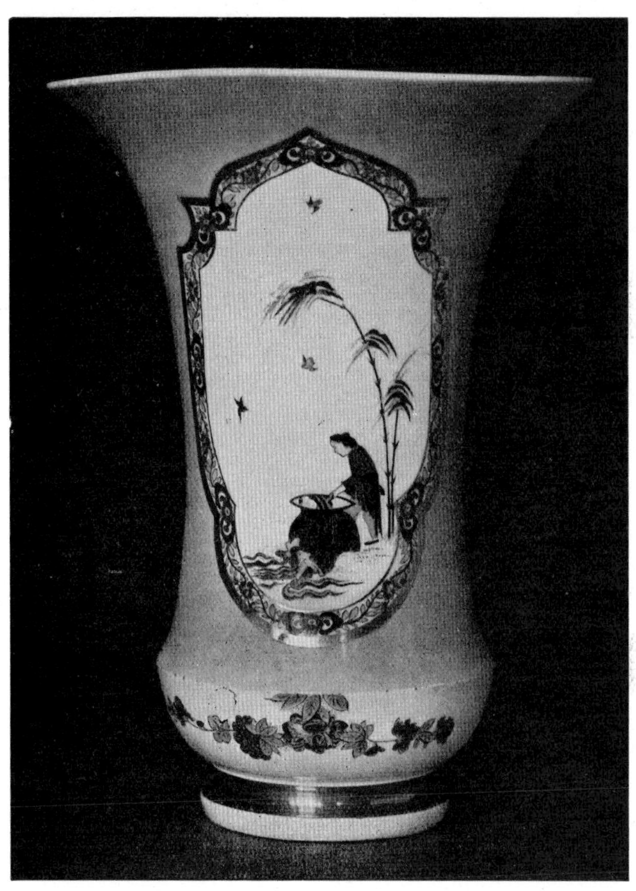

FIG. 29. REVERSE OF VASE SHOWN IN FIG. 28
Painted by A. F. von Löwenfinck. See p. 149.
Frankfort-on-the-Main, Kunstgewerbemuseum

region, until in 1771 ample beds of excellent kaolin were discovered north of Hall. These are still being worked at the time of writing. After the death of Meyer (1785) the further development of modelling at Berlin was due to the efforts of

FIG. 30. TRAY OF A WRITING-SET PAINTED WITH HARBOUR SCENES

Meissen; 1735

Hamburg, Museum für Kunst und Gewerbe

FIG. 31. BELL, INK-POT, AND SAND-POT BELONGING TO THE TRAY SHOWN IN FIG. 30
Meissen; 1735
Hamburg Museum für Kunst und Gewerbe

the architect Hans Christian Genelli, and Gottfried Schadow. J. C. F. Riese was working as head modeller from 1789 to 1834.

In 1753 the ducal factory of Brunswick was founded at Fürstenberg with the help of Johann Benckgraff, who had previously been working at Höchst. At the same time the painter Zeschinger and the modeller Feilner migrated from Höchst. With Feilner as modellers were Johann Christian Rombrich, working from 1762 to 1794, Anton Carl Luplau, from 1776—he was later at Copenhagen—the Frenchman Desoches (1769–74), and Carl Gottlieb Schubert (1775–1804). Here too Passau earth was used at first, until satisfactory kaolin beds were discovered in the neighbourhood. Since 1859 the factory has been a private concern.

In 1755 the Elector Charles Theodore of the Palatinate granted a licence to Paul Hannong, a Strasburg faience- and porcelain-manufacturer, to set up a factory at Frankenthal. Hannong had learned the formula through a migrant from Höchst, Christian von Löwenfinck, a brother of the Adam Friedrich von Löwenfinck mentioned above, and he was making porcelain at Strasburg from 1751 to 1753. Under the monopoly of the French State factory at Vincennes (later Sèvres) any other manufacture of porcelain in France was forbidden, a prohibition which was extended to the territory of Alsace, then known as *étranger effectif*. In consequence Hannong transferred his entire porcelain manufacture to Frankenthal, with models and raw materials and his staff of craftsmen and artists. He himself kept on his faience factory at Strasburg, and left his two sons to manage the concern at Frankenthal. Later on, from 1759 to 1762, his second son, Joseph Adam Hannong, ran the factory on his own account. In spite of large subsidies from the Elector he failed to show a profit, and sold the factory to the Elector, himself returning to Alsace. Adam Bergdoll, a moulder and book-keeper who had been employed at Höchst, was appointed director, and after his departure the post was held by Simon Feilner, of Fürstenberg, who had been working since 1770 as head modeller at Frankenthal. After the occupation of the Palatinate by the French (1795) the factory was leased to Peter von Recum, and ceased work in 1800. Artists of distinction were employed at Frankenthal, especially under the directorship of Bergdoll. Of the painters the most notable were

FIG. 32. TUREEN WITH THE ARMS OF PHILIP CHARLES, ELECTOR OF MAINZ
Meissen; about 1735–40
Frankfort-on-the-Main, Kunstgewerbemuseum

Winterstein, Magnus of Höchst, and Osterspey. The most important modellers were Lanz, whom Hannong had brought with him from Strasburg, and then Johann Friedrich Lück (from about 1757), Karl Gottlieb Lück, and especially the Court statuary Konrad Linck (from 1762 to 1766 at Frankenthal, then at Mannheim, but subsequently working for this factory). Like Kändler at Meissen, Bustelli at Nymphenburg,

Melchior at Höchst, he gave the plastic art of his factory the impress of his own style.

The case of Ludwigsburg is again characteristic. The porcelain factory here had been originally founded by private enterprise, but two years later, in 1758, the management was taken over by Charles Eugene, Duke of Württemberg, who regarded it as "a necessary appanage of lustre and prestige."

FIG. 33. DISH FROM A SERVICE MADE FOR CLEMENT AUGUSTUS, ELECTOR OF COLOGNE
Meissen; about 1740
Mannheim, Hermannsdorf Collection

In the following year he gave the post of director to the expert Joseph Jakob Ringler, whom we have already met at Vienna and at Nymphenburg-Neudeck. A special difficulty here, and a source of great expense, as in most of the other German factories, was the absence of local china-clay and the necessity of fetching it from the Passau district. For the position of head painter an invitation was sent to Gottlieb Friedrich Riedel (1759–79), who had been working hitherto at Meissen, Höchst, and Frankenthal, but now did plastic designs as well. Of the modellers mention may be made of Johann Göz (1760–62), Johann Jakob Louis (1762–72), and Domenico

Ferretti (about 1764–67); but the most important plastic artist and the most typical of the work of the Ludwigsburg factory was Wilhelm Beyer, who worked there from about 1764 to 1767, and then migrated to Vienna. Besides Beyer there were Pierre François Lejeune (*b.* 1721, *d.* 1790) and Johann Heinrich Schmidt (1766–1821). During the later period both the statuaries Dannecker and Scheffauer executed models for the factory, which was dissolved in 1824.

The eight factories cited hitherto, including Vienna, were artistically and materially the most flourishing enterprises in Germany. Besides these there was a whole crop of new foundations which sprang up throughout the second half of the eighteenth century. They have not the same decisive importance for the general history of German porcelain, but in their own way most of them produced quite respectable work, in some cases work of real distinction. We give here a short synopsis of these factories.

In 1758 appeared the Hesse-Darmstadt factory at Kelsterbach on the Main. Its head modeller was Antonius Seefried, who had been at Nymphenburg and was there again later. At Ansbach, where a faience factory had already been in existence for some time, a porcelain factory was founded in 1758, and four years later was transferred to the Jagdschloss Bruckberg. The art director was Johann Friedrich Kändler, a cousin of the famous Kändler of Meissen. Other Meissen workmen were also employed there. Another modeller was called Laut; he was probably Kändler's successor. The factory was sold in 1807.

In 1763 William Henry, Prince of Nassau-Saarbrücken, engaged a Frenchman, Dominique Pellevé, to start a porcelain factory, situated at Ottweiler. Models for Ottweiler were probably executed by the Bruges statuary Paul Louis Cyfflé, who was then working for the faience factory at Niderviller. The painter, F. Karl Wohlfahrt, was previously employed at Frankenthal and at Zweibrücken, and later at Höchst. In the 1780's the factory went over gradually to the manufacture of stoneware.

The porcelain factory of the Prince-Bishop of Fulda was

founded about 1765 with the help of a workman from the Wegely factory at Berlin—Nicolaus Paul. An excellent paste and delicate painting are features of the work of this factory, which now fetches very high prices. The factory came to an end in 1780. Franz Joachim Hess is mentioned as a modeller. Nicolaus Paul and F. J. Hess later worked for the factory at Kassel, which was in existence from 1766 to 1788. The head

FIG. 34. COFFEE-CUP AND COFFEE-POT
Vienna; second quarter of the eighteenth century
Frankfort-on-the-Main, Kunstgewerbemuseum

modeller, Pahland, and the assembler, Künckler, originally came from Fürstenberg. The Duchy of Pfalz-Zweibrücken acquired its porcelain factory in 1767; it was at first in the Schloss Gutenbrunn and then in Zweibrücken itself. The head modeller, Laurentius Russinger of Höchst, was the first manager, and was followed by the assembler Höckel. The business came to an end about 1775. From about 1771 to 1778 porcelain was made in Baden-Baden by Zacharias Pfalzer of Strasburg, together with stoneware and probably faience also.

It remains to notice lastly the wide distribution of porcelain-manufacture in the Thuringian *Wald*, or forest region. Apart from several later factories which arose about 1800 and cannot be considered here, no less than nine new factories were founded in this district within the space of twenty-five years. These Thuringian factories are a class by themselves, distinct from most of their contemporaries and in marked contrast with the great leading factories. Their whole basis was utilitarian

FIG. 35. TUREEN WITH PATTERN KNOWN AS DULONGS-RELIEFZIERAT
Meissen; about 1750
Hamburg, Museum für Kunst und Gewerbe

rather than decorative. Most other factories owed their existence to the whims of royalty: they could count on large subsidies, and they were producing porcelain *de luxe* for the rich. Importation of raw materials from a distance was characteristic of nearly all of them. The Thuringian factories, on the contrary, were primarily commercial enterprises: they used native china-clay and native sandstone containing quartz, and they procured the necessary fuel, in ample quantities and with little trouble or expense, from the great tracts of forest in the mountains. As a rule the paste of these factories will not bear comparison, for purity and general excellence, with the paste of the big factories. They found their market mainly among the peasants and townsfolk of the district, and consequently they had to produce useful, inexpensive wares, which do not reach a very high level except in one or two factories. Another peculiarity is worth remark. The knowledge of how to make porcelain was not transmitted here, as it was everywhere else, by absconding workmen in direct or indirect contact with Meissen; in several places porcelain was quite definitely and quite independently 'invented' by intelligent research and good luck. We confine ourselves here to brief historical notes, and return occasionally to works of several of these factories, all of which are in existence at the time of writing.

The earliest factory was probably that founded at Gotha in 1757. For most of its history it was in private hands and independent of the Court. It was followed in 1760 by Volkstedt. Here a certain Georg Heinrich Macheleid, formerly a theologian, invented porcelain on his own account. He obtained a privilege from the Prince of Schwarzburg-Rudolstadt, and a kind of joint-stock company was formed, in which the Prince had an interest. From about 1783 the best painter, and also modeller, was a certain Cotta, who had previously worked in various other factories. Before his time the position of modeller was held by Künckler, who has already been discovered at Kassel, and had also worked at Fürstenberg, Berlin, and Veilsdorf. At the time of writing the manufacture is still carrying on in the 'Oldest Volkstedt Porcelain Factory,' and artistically has one of the best reputations among modern porcelain works.

Kloster-Veilsdorf, in Hildburghausen, is so far exceptional in that it was a purely personal and royal foundation. The factory was established in 1760 by Prince Frederick William Eugene of Hildburghausen, who piloted it through all financial and artistic troubles. After a career of thirty years it passed into the hands of a lessee. The modeller Cotta, mentioned already, began his career here in 1778.

In 1764 a porcelain factory was established at Wallendorf (Duchy of Coburg) by a firm in which the experts were two cousins by name of Greiner. Some time earlier, in partnership with a Coburg potter, J. G. Dümmler, they had carried

FIG. 36. TEA-KETTLE AND STAND
Meissen; about 1760
Berlin, Schlossmuseum

out research of their own and had succeeded in reinventing porcelain. The Greiners, an old family of Thuringian glassmakers, played an important part in other places. Gotthelf Greiner, who had been one of the founders of the Wallendorf factory and may claim the lion's share in the invention, started a factory at Limbach in 1772, made it extremely efficient, and in 1792 left it to his five sons. At Limbach (Meiningen) we meet again several workmen—painters, moulders, and modellers—who had been previously employed in other factories (Ludwigsburg, Berlin, Ansbach, Kassel, Veilsdorf, Fürstenberg). But at Limbach, as in most of the other Thuringian factories, these names cannot be referred to definite pieces of porcelain. Some of them were quite indifferent artists. The Duchy of Weimar acquired its porcelain factory, at Ilmenau, in 1777. The factory did not begin to flourish until 1786, when it was leased to Gotthelf Greiner of Limbach. A factory founded at Grossbreitenbach (Schwarzburg-Sondershausen) was bought by G. Greiner five years later. A factory which started at Gera (Reuss) in 1779 was taken over the next year by two brothers Greiner. It was brought into close co-operation with the Volkstedt factory, but later it was again working independently. The last foundation worth mentioning was the factory at Rauenstein (Meiningen), also started by three brothers Greiner.

These brief notes show very clearly the restlessness of painters, modellers, arcanists, and other workmen, and how the various German factories were bound together by a tissue of migration and affinity. But naturally each factory developed its own idiom, according to the taste of its director or the peculiar gifts of its artists; and in figure-modelling especially we may detect the most marked diversity of style in the work of different factories. So much so that, without a highly specialized knowledge, it is often difficult to assign Thuringian figures to the factories of their origin. It is this infinite variety of style that makes the study of German porcelain so extremely interesting.

3. Continental Factories other than German

A book which does not set out to give the full history of individual factories need not devote much space to Continental factories outside Germany; and we shall therefore confine ourselves to bare essentials.

It has already been stated that the Meissen enameller and

gilder Christoph Conrad Hunger, after a short stay at Vienna, went on to Venice. In 1720 a porcelain factory was started in that city. This lasted five years (Vezzi factory). A second factory was established in 1765 by Geminiano Cozzi, and was in existence for half a century. In 1735 a factory was started at Doccia, near Florence, by the Marchese Carlo Ginori with the help of an arcanist from Vienna. But the most important of the Italian factories came into existence in

FIG. 37. CUP AND SAUCER, OF TYPE KNOWN AS TREMBLEUSE, FOR AGED AND SICK PEOPLE
Berlin; about 1765. See pp. 138–139.
Frankfort-on-the-Main, Kunstgewerbemuseum

1736 at Capodimonte, near Naples. It owed its foundation to Charles III (IV), King of the Two Sicilies, whose wife was a Saxon princess. The material used was at first a frit-porcelain (soft-paste) with a tendency to a greenish or yellowish hue. The plastic work is gay and lively in modelling, while the vessels are often decorated in vigorous relief. They have been considerably faked of recent years.

When the King succeeded to the throne of Spain in 1759 he transferred the factory, with nearly all the workmen and artists, to Buen Retiro, near Madrid, where it continued to work, exclusively for the Court, until the death of Charles III in 1789. Besides the magnificent interiors in the palaces of

Portici, Aranjuez, and Madrid (*cf.* Fig. 17), Buen Retiro produced quite remarkable groups and figures in a wonderful creamy paste. They are among the best products of European porcelain-modelling, but unfortunately are very little known, being extremely rare (Fig. 199). At Naples a new factory was founded by Ferdinand IV, son of Charles III, in 1771 and continued until 1821. Here there is evidence of strong Vienna influence; in painting and modelling the factory adopted the full classical style. Large biscuit figures after the antique, and vessels with copies of Roman wall-painting and Greek vase-painting, were the chief productions of this factory.

The numerous porcelain factories founded in France, some of them before Böttger's invention, did not produce a true, hard porcelain, but a soft, glassy frit-porcelain. Of these mention may be made of Rouen, Saint-Cloud, Mennecy, and Chantilly. The beautiful yellowish substance of this soft-paste porcelain (*pâte tendre*) has great similarity with *blanc de Chine* (p. 44), and Oriental shapes were eagerly copied in the French factories.

All these establishments, however, were far surpassed by the Vincennes factory, founded in 1740. In 1745 it was turned into a joint-stock company, and in 1753 received the title "Manufacture Royale des Porcelaines de France." In 1756 it was transferred to Sèvres, where it has remained ever since, and in 1759 was taken under royal management by Louis XV. The soft porcelain of Sèvres is quite different from German, both as a chemical composition and as a plastic medium. It developed artistic values of its own; and developed them for the most part from its technical premises. The very soft material required the shapes made from it to be as plain and simple as possible. On the other hand, the easily fused glaze admitted a wonderful repertory of coloured grounds which in depth and brilliance surpass all the grounds of German hard porcelain. The colours of the painted decoration are absorbed by the easily fused glaze, and have such a luminous brilliance that they almost give the impression of underglaze painting. The soft glaze, with its tendency to fracture, and the exorbitant prices made Sèvres vessels of little use for general purposes, and the factory therefore specialized in luxury wares, vases, trinkets, and expensive services for the upper ranks of society. After the discovery of rich beds of kaolin near Limoges in 1768 Sèvres gradually went over to the produc-

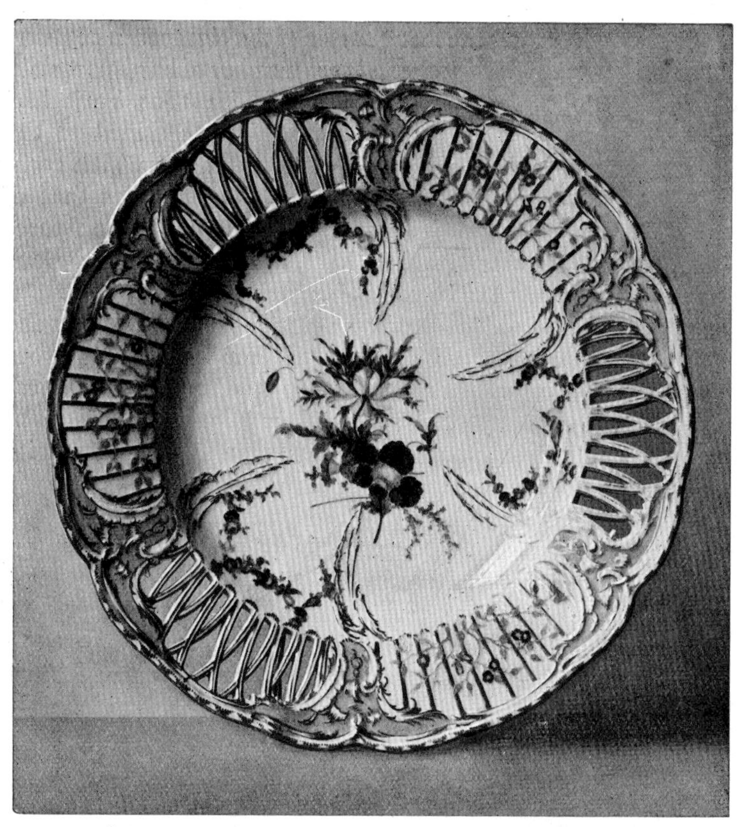

FIG. 38. DESSERT PLATE FROM A SERVICE MADE FOR THE NEW PALACE
Berlin; about 1768
Frankfort-on-the-Main, Kunstgewerbemuseum

tion of hard porcelain, but its style was still determined by the qualities of *pâte tendre*. The technical defects of the soft glaze had a decisive effect on figure-modelling, and led to the production of figures in unglazed biscuit. Delightful figures and groups in biscuit were being made as early as the 1750's, some of them after designs by Boucher. From 1757 Falconet was the director of the modellers, and models for Sèvres biscuit were also executed by Pigalle, Clodion, and other famous artists. The monopoly of the State factory, which had brought Hannong's factory at Strasburg to a standstill, was gradually broken down during the last quarter of the eighteenth century. There arose one after another a large number of hard-porcelain factories in France, especially in Paris (in 1805 Paris had twenty-seven factories), almost all of them confined to the manufacture of vessels. The one French factory which competed with Sèvres in the production of figures was that of Niderviller, in Lorraine (from 1768). Extremely fine figures of faience were also produced there, and in delicacy of glaze and painting were a close rival of porcelain (*cf.* Fig. 193).

The Zürich porcelain factory was established in 1763 at the instance of the poet and painter Salomon Gessner; Gessner himself had a hand in the painting of vessels. The technical expert of the factory, Johann Adam Spengler, of Schaffhausen, had brought his knowledge with him from Höchst. In spite of the artistic excellence of its work the factory failed to overcome its financial troubles, and the manufacture of porcelain ceased soon after 1800. Porcelain was also made at Nyon, on the Lake of Geneva, following the Paris style and with floral decoration, much of it rather tedious.

At Tournai, in Belgium, soft porcelain was made in the style of Sèvres, while hard porcelain was produced in several Dutch factories founded with the help of German workmen—Weesp, Oude Loosdrecht (later Oude Amstel), and The Hague—but it did not achieve any great importance.

Finally we may mention the Danish and Russian factories. After various unsuccessful experiments hard porcelain was first produced at Copenhagen in the year 1773. The factory, at first a joint-stock company, was taken over by the State. A number of leading modellers and painters were collected from German factories. In consequence of the lateness of its foundation Copenhagen scarcely worked at all in the rococo style, but followed the stream of the classical revival. An example is provided by the refrigerator from the Flora Danica

FIG. 39. TEA AND COFFEE SET FOR TWO (TÊTE-À-TÊTE) PAINTED WITH BIRDS
Berlin; about 1770
Frankfort-on-the-Main, Kunstgewerbemuseum

service, painted between 1790 and 1802 (Fig. 86). The plastic work of the factory is often of fine quality, and sometimes shows the influence of Fürstenberg; the group in Fig. 198 is an example of it. The Fürstenberg modeller Anton Carl Luplau was employed at Copenhagen. Of several

FIG 40. PLUTO AND CERBERUS, PROBABLY ALLEGORICAL OF EARTH AND ONE OF A SET OF THE ELEMENTS, AND A LADY WITH A BASKET
Derby; about 1750
London, Victoria and Albert Museum

porcelain factories founded in Russia we need mention only one here, that of St Petersburg (Leningrad); artistically it did not reach a very high standard.

4. English Porcelain Factories

The present section anticipates in several respects the account of porcelain technique which follows, but now that the source and progress of European porcelain have been described we may turn aside at this point to follow the effluence which leads to England. No one who is acquainted with German porcelain or with some of the work of Sèvres will make large claims for the English factories. Their art was transmitted to them. They lacked the sympathy for their stuff which Meissen had for her hard-paste, the Venetians for soda-glass, any creator for the medium which he has created. There was little invention in their style. They had an earnest desire to be Continental, and in fulfilling it they lost the sense of decoration which is evident in the native pottery of England. Their adventures into fashion produced mainly ornamentation; a feeling for decoration appears only in minor factories like New Hall, which were not aware of Europe. In this respect *chinoiserie* was the opportunity which they used best; it meant so little to them that they could do with it what they pleased. They lost as well as gained by thus being themselves. The Germans revered porcelain almost as the Chinese revered jade, but in England porcelain was never *precious*, and the English factories continued to make and throw and model it with an earthen mind. The Longton Hall model of a boy in Fig. 44 is a charming instance of a 'Staffordshire figure' which happens to be porcelain.

FIG. 41. VASE PAINTED IN THE KAKIEMON STYLE
Bow; about 1755
London, Victoria and Albert Museum

But on the whole there is no modelling in English porcelain, as Kändler and Bustelli figures are indeed modelling. Porcelain plastic in Germany sprang from a tradition of baroque sculpture, and as soon as the 'sculptors' had learned the difference between hewing and modelling the German factories did great things; they had a sense of form behind them. In England there was no such tradition, and what there was scarcely trickled into porcelain. One or two notable sculptors have been connected with it, but they did nothing memorable;

and by the time Flaxman appeared that old villain Wedgwood had put his foot down. As for a tradition in modelling, Dwight of Fulham had produced some baroque figures in stoneware, but they were without issue. The early pottery figures contemporary with those in porcelain sometimes have the 'shrinkage' of good modelling, and they are occasionally composed, but they gave little form to the sister art. French fashion was too strong. In plastic work the English factories maintained themselves mainly by copying or adapting from French and German models, paintings, engravings, and they frequently did so without analysing and recomposing the original. The group *Pensent-ils au Raisin?* in Fig. 59 is a good rococo theme, and an opportunity lost by slovenly composition.

FIG. 42. CUP AND SAUCER
Bow; about 1755
London, Victoria and Albert Museum

But if English porcelain is not much of an art by Meissen standards it is, at least, a local idiom with some pleasant expressions. Chelsea may be admired for giving her rococo a metropolitan success (Fig. 48) and an English flavour (Fig. 49). Bow has won a general affection by her engaging incompetence (Fig. 43). Cookworthy porcelain wears a worried look, having more ambition than ability (Figs. 54, 55). At Lowestoft there is neatness and an East Anglian contentment. Longton Hall is Chelsea in Staffordshire, potters' porcelain. Worcester invested her good tradesmanship in the mildness—and the grandness—of a ball at Bath. Sweetness and a Midland vulgarity are the characteristics of Derby. Where Worcester had at least decorated her vessels with French engravings Derby liked to hang a 'Grecian' vase with an English water-colour. And north of Derby there is no porcelain to speak of.

If these factory personalities have a common character it is an English regardlessness, which keeps breaking in upon the most French endeavours. A nationality which is almost originality is evident in most of the illustrations which accompany this section, and there is no need to particularize; but perhaps the best instance is that of the inscribed flasks and

FIG. 43. LADY WITH A MANDOLIN AND MAN WITH A FIDDLE
Bow; about 1750
London, Victoria and Albert Museum

trinkets known as Chelsea 'toys.' They were invented by a Frenchman in England, but they have regardlessness, and that may well be the reason why they are so well recognized on the Continent. They are English porcelain, just as Byron was an English 'milord' and the English poet. Besides regardlessness there was prudence—a desire to fortify the body of porcelain and make it marketable, and it was this which led ultimately to the triumph of the bone-ash tradition in England.

To discover how this idiom grew one must begin with

trade rather than with art. There was little patronage in English porcelain or proud emulation of the prince next door. George II and the Duke of Cumberland had, it is true, some interest in Chelsea, but as a rule the owners of the English factories were plain men of middle station looking for a living in the new fashion from abroad. They began with luxuries for the nobility and ended in ware for every one. English porcelain lost a good deal by this lack of endowment. There was not the infinite patience in experiment which only an income can sustain, nor the perfect 'complexion' that princes demanded. There was not the same search for artists of talent who might be hired into the porcelain factories and lose themselves in a programme. Nor was there, in the public, the critical appetite and the sense of prestige which made German porcelain a royal art. English porcelain made Wedgwood's distinction; the 'ornamental' minority of Chelsea and her disciples observed the modes of a small and elegant world. In the hands of the majority the intentions of Bow became the idiom of England—"a more ordinary sort of ware for common uses."

FIG. 44. FIGURE OF A BOY
Longton Hall; about 1755
London, Victoria and Albert Museum

The idiom which began in private enterprise was continued into the chemistry of the porcelain bodies. There are four technical traditions among the English factories; the French, or soft-paste, tradition of Chelsea, early Derby, and Longton Hall; the bone-ash tradition of Bow and Lowestoft and the factories which it conquered at a later date; Cookworthy's

Fountain, with Figure of a Woman
By F. A. Bustelli. Nymphenburg; about 1760
Munich, Bayerisches National-Museum

hard-paste tradition at Plymouth, Bristol, and New Hall; and the Western, or soapstone, tradition of Worcester and her 'colonies.' In a general sense it is true that the four bodies entailed four styles in an artistic sense. By the time these four traditions had worked themselves out England was left with a standard porcelain body; the winner was bone-ash.

FIG 45. PLATE PAINTED WITH BIRDS
Longton Hall; about 1755
London, Victoria and Albert Museum

In the remaining part of this section I can only refer very briefly to the careers of these factories.

The Soft-paste Tradition. The date of the foundation of Chelsea porcelain factory is not known, but certain dated pieces prove that the factory was in existence in 1745. The first proprietor, Charles Gouyn, was probably a Frenchman; he was succeeded about 1749 by a Soho silversmith Nicholas Sprimont, also of French extraction. The factory was encouraged by the Duke of Cumberland, and lived on the market provided by the Court and the wealthier society of London. In the earlier part of its career the work of the factory may be described as imitation of Meissen in a French paste. The body at first was very soft and vitreous, and more creamy than white in colour. It resembles the paste of Saint-Cloud porcelain, and Gouyn or one of his assistants may well have learned the composition at that factory. This paste could not be modelled very accurately and was unsatisfactory in the kiln. About 1750 it was replaced by another body of the same general type, but of a much whiter complexion and of a stronger constitution; even Chelsea had to think of utility. The improved body at its best is among the finest soft-pastes ever produced. As a medium for modelling and firing figures it was superior to its French contemporaries, and it may well have been introduced because Chelsea wished to copy Kändler and other German figures, but could not do so in her early paste; there could be no Kändler style at Saint-Cloud. About 1760 there was a reassertion of French influence, but in style rather than in chemistry; models, shapes, colours, schemes of decoration, were copied from Sèvres, and themes were freely adapted from French rococo painting, particularly from Boucher.

Sprimont continued to be manager of the Chelsea works until 1769, and he may fairly be regarded as the creator of Chelsea toys, which have done more perhaps than anything else to make the name of Chelsea famous on the Continent. Sprimont gave up his position in 1769 on account of ill-health. In the following year the factory was bought by William Duesbury, of Derby, an aggressive provincial who was determined to succeed. Under Duesbury's direction the factory continued operations until 1784, in which year it was closed. The productions of this period are commonly known as Chelsea-Derby (1770–84), but the hand of Duesbury was upon them. The figures especially are more Derby than Chelsea, and combine a degraded Boucher sentiment with the first symptoms of the classical revival.

But Chelsea, metropolitan Chelsea, has always taken first place among the English factories, and deserves it. In her market, her rococo, and not least in her art she will bear comparison with the great factories of Germany and France, and it would be difficult to make the same claim for any of her compatriots. Her earlier figures are perhaps the best index of her attainment. They may not be original, but they are at least modelled, sometimes better modelled than their German prototypes. Tradition has connected her name with

FIG. 46. LEDA AND THE SWAN
Adapted from a painting by F. Boucher. Chelsea; about 1755
London, Victoria and Albert Museum

that of the distinguished sculptor L. F. Roubiliac, and however far tradition may be true in fact, it is at least true to the character of Chelsea.

The factory at Longton Hall was the first to continue the Chelsea tradition outside London. Its owner, William Littler, was a salt-glaze potter, and appears as such in his porcelain. This he began to make about 1752, and continued to do so until 1759, when the factory is believed to have been bought by Duesbury. The paste was soft, translucent, and vitreous,

FIG. 47. FIGURE OF A REAPER, PROBABLY ALLEGORICAL OF SUMMER AND ONE OF A SET OF THE SEASONS
Chelsea; about 1760
London, Victoria and Albert Museum

like the early paste of Chelsea, and it is conceivable that William Littler, potter, obtained the help of a Chelsea workman when he set about the manufacture of porcelain. It was a courageous act for a solitary man in the heart of the earthenware country. Staffordshire was not very receptive of foreign ideas, and the taste for porcelain was still to be created. For a factory like Littler's there were two paths to success. One was to vulgarize rococo as Duesbury did, the other was to produce good sound ware. Littler made some

FIG. 48. TOILET-MIRROR AND STAND
Chelsea; about 1760
London, Victoria and Albert Museum

attempt to strengthen the body in the direction of Worcester, but in the end he fell between the two stools of a Chelsea paste and a provincial market. In its style this little factory was never provincial as Derby was, but local; that is its isolated charm. In the figures (*e.g.*, Fig. 44) and the leaf dishes it is easy to see that the potter's idiom would not be denied.

The precise origin of porcelain-manufacture at Derby is still obscure, but marked and dated pieces prove that porcelain was being made there as early as 1750. The most important name connected with the Derby factory is that of William Duesbury, a commercial upstart and a perfect Arnold Bennett character. He was the son of a currier of Cannock, and seems to have begun his career at Longton, but by 1751 he had established himself in London as a free-lance enameller (*Hausmaler*; *cf.* p. 125). He painted Chelsea, Bow, and other porcelains for London dealers; he was thus well acquainted with their pastes, and had his finger on the movement of fashion. He knew 'the trade' and knew 'the market' as a detached manufacturer never can, and he financed his knowledge and his enterprise by a knack of extracting money from others. He got his father's savings by a one-sided promise, and in John Heath, banker of Derby, he found a moneyed mute who was willing to become his partner. His cue was to step in on the failures of other men and make them a commercial success. He did so at Longton Hall in 1759, at Chelsea in 1770, at Bow in 1776; and when he took a hand at Derby in 1756 it may be that he saw an opportunity in the impotence of an earlier manufacture. He knew exactly what would sell; and Chelsea offered the snob appeal so important for creating a market. Duesbury, knowing Chelsea, concluded that it was a more paying game to vulgarize Chelsea than to create a sound agreeable ware like Worcester, and we may suspect that in the earlier part of his career at Derby he was making Chelsea porcelain in the Midlands and painting it up in his London workshop. When Chelsea and rococo were on the wane Duesbury 'went out' at precisely the right moment, and invested with great acumen in a new and promising stock which is now called classicism. Chelsea-Derby (1770–84) was Duesbury's transition, and the paste changed with the style from a Chelsea soft-paste to a bone-ash porcelain.

Rococo had been too good a style for him, but in classicism he was entirely at home, and as that style came into the ascendant he gathered about him a body of modellers and painters who made late Derby the best classical porcelain in England. The most notable modellers were J. J. Spengler, of Zürich, Stephan, and Coffee. Among his painters Zachariah Boreman and William Billingsley may be regarded as the leaders of a 'water-colour' school. Late Derby is in a sense the only *Derby* porcelain. In Duesbury's concerns the man,

FIG. 49. PLATE OF TYPE SIMILAR TO THE SERVICE GIVEN BY GEORGE III AND QUEEN CHARLOTTE TO THE DUKE OF MECKLENBURG-STRELITZ IN 1763
Chelsea; about 1760–65
London, Victoria and Albert Museum

not the factory, was the dynamic unity; early Derby, Chelsea-Derby, and late Longton are all Duesbury porcelain. Duesbury died appropriately in 1786, at the height of the classical revival; *si monumentum requiris*, there are the white biscuit figures. Porcelain continued to be made at Derby, by Bloor and others, but there is some excuse for taking leave of it at Duesbury's death.

The Bone-ash Tradition. Homage is due to the slighted Bow factory for inventing the body which conquered all England;

whereas Chelsea is the greatest English factory, Bow is the most significant. The factory was founded in 1744 by Edward Heylyn, copper merchant, and Thomas Frye, painter and mezzotinter. At first the partners used a clay imported from America ("the produce of the Chirokee nation . . . called by the natives unaker"), but with this they could produce only a coarse and impracticable soft-paste. Four years later Frye had overcome these early difficulties, and took out the famous Second Bow Patent for a bone-ash porcelain made by

FIG. 50. SAUCER PAINTED IN LILAC AND TEAPOT PAINTED IN BLACK
Worcester; about 1760
London, Victoria and Albert Museum

calcining "all animal substances, all fossils of the calcareous kind such as chalk, limestone, etc." The resulting paste had many defects, but it served its purpose. Frye was neither a potter nor a professional chemist, but an artist, and his porcelain is distinguished by a natural good taste which would not be bothered with chemical fuss, and was in some sense independent of contemporary fashion. Of course, he used rococo, and he copied Meissen figures, but he did not try to beat Chelsea at her own game. He created a market for pleasant table wares, and his bone-ash paste was just good enough. Bow figures and Bow rococo have a guileless charm which has become her chief reputation, but her most characteristic and important work is to be found in her table wares and her *chinoiserie*. Chinese porcelain-painting and especially the Japanese Kakiemon style were not merely 'quaint,' but good decoration for ordinary vessels, and Frye may be given much credit for fitting his paste to 'wares of common use' and his decoration to his market.

Frye continued in control of Bow until 1759, and died in

FIG. 51. COFFEE-POT TRANSFER-PRINTED IN BLACK WITH A SUBJECT KNOWN AS L'AMOUR
From a plate by R. Hancock after a French original. Worcester; about 1765.
London, Victoria and Albert Museum

1762. The business was carried on by two partners who had joined the firm in 1750, but the survivor, John Crowther, became bankrupt in 1762. The factory continued working till 1776, when it was absorbed by the omnivorous Duesbury.

The bone-ash tradition made its first excursion into the provinces in 1757, when a factory was started at Lowestoft by one Robert Browne and a company. There is a story that Browne discovered the Bow method of making porcelain by getting a job at the factory, but in the eighteenth century all ceramic secrets were discovered in this way, and the story may well mean that Browne was simply a Bow workman with

FIG. 52. VASE PAINTED WITH BIRDS IN GILT ROCOCO PANELS RESERVED IN A GROUND OF DARK BLUE SCALE PATTERN
Worcester; about 1770
London, Victoria and Albert Museum

ambitions. The story is confirmed by evidence of paste, style, and 'market.' When bone-ash fared forth into East Anglia it left the spirit of rococo, even Bow rococo, behind it. It brought with it an inclination to be useful and a preference for Chinese decoration.

Lowestoft, lacking all pretensions, gained both neatness and spontaneity. The former quality is evident in her cups and saucers, teapots, and other wares, which are sometimes patronized as 'cottage china.' Borders derived from Chinese porcelain were happily combined with natural flowers, and when she turned to figured subjects and scenes she produced an indolent rural *chinoiserie* which escapes being any conven-

FIG. 53. DISH PAINTED IN COLOURS WITH A LAKE SCENE REMINISCENT OF THE CHINESE
Bow; about 1770
London, Victoria and Albert Museum

tion but her own. She is the most absent-minded of factories, and stayed in little habits of rococo long after the great world had gone on into classicism. With this unpunctual charm she had few interests, and in large quantities she is an awful bore; but she produced the ideal china for a late breakfast.

The factory was a small one, and had an uneventful career of nearly half a century. Lowestoft has given her name to the large quantities of porcelain which were made in China to English orders, but in view of Lowestoft style the misnomer ('Chinese Lowestoft') is easy to explain.

Bone-ash paste subsequently passed to several factories which have been or will be noticed on their initial characters.

Chelsea adopted it in 1758, Derby in 1770, Worcester, Pinxton, Coalport, in the last decade of the eighteenth century. Finally it made its way into Staffordshire, which before the nineteenth century was not primarily porcelain country, and in the hands of Staffordshire potters it became the accepted porcelain of all England. Bone-ash porcelain is not a matter for national pride, but of its importance in history there can be little doubt.

The Soapstone Tradition of the West. For a time bone-ash por-

FIG. 54. VENUS AND ADONIS WITH CUPID, AND A SHEPHERD AND SHEPHERDESS
Bristol; about 1770
London, Victoria and Albert Museum

celain, as a fortified soft-paste, had a rival in a West-of-England body made from soapstone (steatite). The 'soapy rock,' as Dr Pococke called it, was found in Cornwall, and its career as a fortifier took a natural course—Bristol, Worcester, Caughley (Shropshire), and Liverpool. It never got a footing in the Midlands. Duesbury of Derby had the offer of it and even tried it, but he shrewdly preferred bone-ash; freight costs must be considered. Soapstone porcelain was first made at Bristol as early as 1750 at 'Lowdin's China House,' premises attached to a glass-house and taken by a company for the manufacture of porcelain. Who brought the soapstone to Bristol is not certain, but we may suspect William Cookworthy, apothecary of Plymouth. Cookworthy had been rambling in Cornwall in 1745, searching for ingredients, perhaps at the suggestion of Heylyn and Frye, and if he was "the first inventor of the Bristol china works," Lowdin's porcelain may be regarded as a Cookworthy experiment and the prelude to hard-paste. Apparently the experiment did not pay, for in 1752 it was acquired by a much more powerful combination and moved up the Severn water-way to Worcester. Lowdin porcelain is early Worcester. The paste, for

FIG. 55. FOUR FIGURES ALLEGORICAL OF THE ELEMENTS
Bristol; modelled about 1772
London, Victoria and Albert Museum

a soft-paste, is distinctly hard, a quality which it lost on migration. The Lowdin style has an air of eclectic indecision, as if the proprietors never worked up their programme; many of the shapes were, for example, imitated from silver. Lowdin's China House, in fact, was not a factory, but a laboratory which tried for a year or two to pay for its researches; its chemist surely was Cookworthy.

Its offspring at Worcester is a good instance of collective enterprise. The factory was founded in 1751 by the subscriptions of "fifteen gentlemen" and the enterprise of Dr John Wall, physician of Worcester. The chemist was an apothecary by name William Davis, who had probably learned his paste at the Lowdin laboratory. Soapstone porcelain was already being made before Dr Wall's company acquired the Bristol plant, and it was not superseded for nearly fifty years. Cathedral nostrils must not be assailed by thoughts of a bone mill, whereas soapstone (which Duesbury rejected) was a nice clean mineral from the sea. It well served the purpose of fifteen gentlemen who, avoiding all meanness, expected,

FIG. 56. THE 'RANELAGH FIGURES'
Derby; about 1760
London, Victoria and Albert Museum

nevertheless, interest on their subscriptions. If your factory is endowed by a potentate there is no need to worry if your teacups collapse at tea; wasters are allowed for in the estimates, and you need only wait on the favour of the kiln. Soapstone removed anxiety and ensured a market. By its aid the fifteen gentlemen carried their pleasant, reliable, gentlemanly porcelain into the Hall and the Parsonage of the Western shires. It was china proper to a Jane Austen world.

Time was not important in the West of England, and

Worcester used this fact to singular advantage. No factory has such independence of style or has expressed the English character so successfully in porcelain. Her achievement was not simply an accident of geography, but the consequence of a policy. London fashions arrived late; the scramble for primacy was just beginning beyond the Cotswolds when it was just ending among the ladies of London. Worcester had to use

FIG. 57. THREE DERBY FIGURES

Left, John Wilkes with *Magna Charta*, the Bill of Rights, and Locke's essay on government; about 1775. *Centre*, the actor James Quin as Falstaff; about 1765. *Right*, General Conway; about 1775.

London, Victoria and Albert Museum

the instinct for novelties—it was more potent in quiet and remote places—but she did not try to be always up-to-date. She found a cleverer means of *selling* the porcelain which was to wear well. By the aid of French engravings adapted by Robert Hancock and transfer-printed on to porcelain Worcester created a fiction of modernity, and gave vicarage ladies a sense of Paris. Hancock's *Amusements* were in impeccable taste and had a pretty sentiment. They were not just put on, but really adapted to porcelain as engravings were adapted in Germany; in the most pedantic sense they were 'ceramic' ornament. They easily kept their market interested by an occasional new subject. Above all they cost little to the producer, and could be reproduced by the hundred. The discreet shopkeeping which had elected soapstone porcelain now appeared upon its surface.

Worcester, of course, had other styles. The shiftlessness of Lowdin silver forms she turned into ' county ' rococo. She had some charming *chinoiserie* and excellent painters. Towards 1770 she had an attack of Chelsea, and used it well for the benefit of the Hall, producing her famous 'coloured grounds,' with exotic and dishevelled birds. But among these and many other diversities the transfer-printed wares remain the epitome of Worcester and of English porcelain. Where other porcelains exploited fashion these were an authentic enterprise in taste in the same sense as early Meissen.

Dr Wall died in 1776, and for seven years afterwards the factory was carried on by William Davis. In 1783 the original company was dissolved, and the factory was bought by its London agent, Thomas Flight. It remained in his and his partner's families until 1840. A second factory was established at Worcester in 1786 by Robert Chamberlain, and remained in his family until 1840, when it amalgamated with the senior factory. Little need be said of their works; the genius of Worcester died with Dr Wall. Thereafter the factory lost itself in classical design and pictorial landscape, and so fell into a jargon common to every one.

Soapstone porcelain was too individual a thing to fare well in other hands. Some time before 1756 a Liverpool potter, Richard Chaffers, seems to have learned to make the soapstone body from a Robert Podmore, who had worked under Davis at Worcester. Chaffers' intentions were merely commercial. He had a soapstone quarry in Cornwall, and he probably acquired it in order to supply his porcelain manufactory with cheap sea-borne soapstone. He carefully tested his teacups in hot water. He copied Worcester transfer-prints, and had them executed by a firm of hack decorators. He occasionally had a good painter in his employ, but for the most part he tore the tradesmanship out of Worcester's book and left the quality behind.

Caughley, on the other hand, was rank imitation, and bad

imitation at that. The manufacture of porcelain was begun in 1772 by Thomas Turner, an assistant of Hancock, who had

FIG. 58. VASE WITH DECORATION PAINTED IN COLOURS IN A SÈVRES STYLE

Perhaps by a Frenchman 'Soqui.' Bristol; about 1775.

London, Victoria and Albert Museum

a knowledge of the Worcester paste, and had married the daughter of a Caughley potter. Turner's factory was acquired in 1799 by one of its own apprentices, John Rose, who had founded a factory at Coalport, on the other side of the Severn; and it ceased working in 1814. For a time Rose used a soapstone body, but he eventually adopted the prevailing bone-

FIG. 59. GROUP AFTER AN ENGRAVING BY J. P. LE BAS OF A PAINTING BY F. BOUCHER ENTITLED "PENSENT-ILS AU RAISIN?"
Chelsea-Derby; about 1775
London, Victoria and Albert Museum

ash. So ended the soapstone tradition. If Bow is important for her posterity, Worcester stands on her own achievement.

Hard-paste Porcelain. William Cookworthy, apothecary of Plymouth and friend of admirals, is the English Böttger, the only man in English porcelain with the faith and patience of alchemy. We have suggested that Lowdin's China House was

Cookworthy's laboratory; when it passed to Worcester in 1752 Cookworthy went home. Nothing happened for sixteen years. Soapstone porcelain was not good enough; by 1755 he had found china-clay (kaolin), but there was still petuntse,

FIG. 60. CUPS AND SAUCERS, TEAPOT, AND CREAM-JUGS PAINTED IN COLOURS
Lowestoft; late eighteenth century
London, Victoria and Albert Museum

or china-stone. The last ingredient of true porcelain was still to win. One can picture Cookworthy during this long eclipse, poring over the letters of Père d'Entrecolles or poking about in Cornish strata with the curious intensity of science. By 1768 he had succeeded. He had found petuntse, he had reproduced the glaze of Ching-tê Chên, and he had produced a true

Chinese porcelain for the first and only time in England. His patent was taken out on March 17, and he already had a company waiting to use it. For two years the manufacture was carried on at Plymouth, but several of his company were Bristol men, and in 1770 the factory was transferred to Castle Green in that city.

Bristol porcelain was a great triumph, but not a great success. Cookworthy never learned, he never had time to learn, to mix his ingredients, and Bristol paste, with its cracks and bendings, its gritty accretions, its smoky glaze, has all the air of a *doctrinaire* porcelain. If Cookworthy had had a long experience in producing in a factory what he heroically invented we may think that he would have cured these imperfections. But he suffered the common fate of inventors, that of inventing in any interest but his own. When the infant hard-paste was put out to nurse at Bristol Cookworthy lost his hold on it; he could no longer observe and educate its daily habits. In 1773 all the rights in it were purchased by one of the company, Richard Champion, a volatile person with the limitations, but none of the thoroughness, of tradesmanship. His name was an unkind irony, for in his hands hard-paste neither perfected its technique nor discovered an art. Figures were made, Derby was admired, classicism was adopted, but Cookworthy porcelain never created a style of its own, worthy of thirty years' preparation and an obvious ambition. It was the tragic dwindling of a famous victory, and it ended in a good 'cottage china' which other factories could do quite as well on a tithe of the experiment and in a different porcelain. Towards 1780 the duffer Champion got into difficulties, and in 1781 sold the patent to a company of Staffordshire potters who thought there might be 'something in it.' The factory was moved to New Hall, and continued to make hard-paste until, about 1810, the doors were opened to the ubiquitous bone-ash.

The 'cottage china' of New Hall was quiet and decorative, but only its body was hard porcelain; its happy thoughts were in the earthenware tradition. When hard-paste moved into Staffordshire two things might have happened. The New

Hall company might have continued the work which Cookworthy had begun, bringing their paste to a Meissen perfection, and discovering for it an art of porcelain. They might have made English porcelain a hard-paste. But Staffordshire was no place for alchemy or for patronage, and the New Hall partners took the other course, reducing their opportunity to the limits of their experience. They were small men, and the main responsibility was not theirs. The question is asked: "Who killed hard-paste?" "I," said Josiah Wedgwood, "with my enlightened self-interest and my cream-coloured earthenware."

FIG. 61. EWER WITH DECORATION PAINTED BY Z. BOREMAN AND R. ASKEW
Derby; about 1780
London, Victoria and Albert Museum

It has only been possible to mention the more important of the English factories, but the rest may be resumed in two persons of significance. One is an individualist, the other stands for an industry and an epoch. William Billingsley (1758–1828) was a romantic flower-painter of the Derby factory, and he spent his life in making a soft white paste with a 'complexion' suitable for painting, and in hawking it about all over England. With his painter's porcelain in his pocket he went to Pinxton, to Mansfield, perhaps to Torksey and Wirksworth, to Worcester, Nantgarw, Swansea, and to Coalport, where he died. He had to find established manufacturers who would believe in his formula, and it was often a broken and hopeless pilgrimage; but on several of these factories he left his mark, and the work of three of them,

FIG. 62. FIGURE OF A BOY, BISCUIT PORCELAIN, MODELLED BY W. COFFEE
Derby; end of the eighteenth century
London, Victoria and Albert Museum

Nantgarw (1811–14 and 1817–19), Swansea (1814–17 and 1817–24), and Coalport (1819–28), may be fairly regarded as Billingsley porcelain. If his naturalism is admitted Billingsley was a good painter, and he understood the value of the white ground in porcelain decoration; but his paste was unstable and his method the old one of putting the cart before the horse. He fitted his paste to his decoration, not his decoration to his paste. His importance is that he contributed much to the making of an all-England mode.

The second person is Josiah Spode II. He stands for Staffordshire and the standard English body of the nineteenth century. In Staffordshire porcelain, as in Staffordshire Bennett, there was both an Enoch and an Arnold. The Enoch produced a working compromise between the idealism of hard-paste and the vulgar utility of bone-ash, did it by dreary prudence and conservative industry. But there was also an Arnold who dreamed of porcelain for 'marble halls' and craved the magnificence of a Grand Babylon Hotel. This union of utilitarian paste with 'Grand Babylon' decoration swept England. In the factories of Spode, Copeland, Coalport, Rockingham, Chamberlain, Bloor, it produced great flamboyant services for a new middle class which was being enriched, but not yet ennobled, by the Industrial Revolution. And as a style in porcelain it is still, astonishingly, with us.

5. Technique and Economy

Before we consider the art of porcelain we must glance at certain conditions of its technique and its economy, since the history of the industry as a whole was determined by them.

The preparation of a good body rarely succeeded at the first attempt; the problems to be solved were long and difficult. The obstacles which Meissen had encountered as pioneer and had overcome by her own efforts were writ small in nearly every other factory; and great importance was therefore attached to the acquisition of good arcanists, on whom the management of the factory largely depended. Hopes were often disappointed; the arcanists were dismissed or went to and fro in secret. In many factories, Ludwigsburg for example, it was some time before the paste was perfected, while the glaze was coarse and yellowish. It was important that there should be no technical defects in the construction of the kiln, since the porcelain was fired at an extremely high temperature with wood fuel. Pit coal was not generally used

FIG. 63. BERLIN CHANDELIER IN THE AUDIENCE CHAMBER OF THE PALACE AT ANSBACH
Photo Stoedtner

until the nineteenth century, although at Ottweiler coal-firing was probably introduced when the factory started. At Meissen in 1720 complaints were made that out of twenty-four dozen cups fired scarcely a dozen were fit to use when they

Tureen painted with Birds and Blue Triangle-diaper
Sèvres; 1759
Munich, Bayerisches National-Museum

came out of the kiln; a fact which shows the great importance to a factory of intelligent technical experts, workmen who understood the proper way to mix the body and the glaze, and firemen who could be trusted to carry out the firing correctly. Even when the firing is correctly conducted there are always some pieces which go wrong. At Meissen, as in other factories, the fired pieces were divided into three classes: good pieces, medium quality, and wasters, or rubbish. The medium wares, being sold at a lower rate, were a constant cause of fakes and perversions, since they were decorated outside the factory by so-called *Hausmaler*, or free-lance painters. Some of their work is now highly valued, but in their day the *Hausmaler* were ostracized and persecuted as 'botchers' and 'bunglers' and painting 'pettifoggers.'[1] The wasters were not usually sold, but given away to workmen and other people connected with the factory.

The greatest care had to be exercised in the selection and training of the other workmen. First comes the so-called 'white gang,' including throwers, moulders, assemblers, and modellers. At the head of them was usually the chief modeller, and their work was finished as soon as the piece came out of the kiln a success. Then the painting gang came into action. The blue-painters painted on the body after firing, and when the glaze was put on their brush strokes united with it to make a single homogeneous weld. On the other hand, the colour-painters, using coloured enamels, did not begin to paint until the glaze had been fired on in the glazing furnace. Their colours were then developed in a third kiln, called the muffle or coffin. The painters were also divided into various groups—flower-painters, landscape-painters, figure-painters, portrait-painters, and so on. Each workman had his own province assigned him, and was trained for it as an apprentice; it was rare for one man to be master of several departments at a time. There were also the decorators (*Staffierer*), whose chief work was to paint the statuettes; they also had to execute the gilding and coloured decoration for certain details of vessels which did not demand great artistic ability.

[1] The epithets were: *Pfuscher*, *Stümpler*, and *Winkelmaler* (at Vienna).

The value or otherwise of the work of a factory was determined always by the capacity of its artists—painters, like Herold of Meissen, as well as modellers. The really notable porcelain-modellers of the eighteenth century can be numbered on the fingers, but besides these there were a number of talented performers, rather overshadowed by their abler colleagues, as well as a host of hacks whose names are not worth conjuring from oblivion. But the work of the best modeller would have been condemned to failure without the clever assembler (*Bossierer, Poussierer*)[1] to help him; for it was the assembler with his sensitive hands who undertook to multiply the model of clay or, occasionally, wood. The reproduction of such a model is by no means an easy task. A hollow plaster mould was made from the model—a very complicated business. The whole group or figure had to be divided into dozens of separate pieces. All these separate parts were copied in the porcelain paste, and then had to be reassembled. The heads, arms, feet, the various attributes and other trimmings, and the base were joined together to make a single whole. The suggested movement of a hand or the exquisite poise of a head is often essential to the final effect of the figure as a work of art; and a clumsy assembler might easily spoil everything by a moment's indecision. Otherwise he enjoyed considerable freedom, and by a different combination of the pieces, or by a permutation of the motives at his disposal, he might produce a most interesting series of variants. We may compare, for example, the different versions of a Fulda model that had been twice reproduced. We may observe, too, how the plastic artist, or modeller, is governed by the peculiar character of his medium. He must always bear in mind that porcelain has a tendency to collapse in the intense heat of the kiln. Figures with outstretched arms are always a risky experiment, since an unsupported arm will probably sag during the firing. If a figure is somewhat heavy, or if flowing draperies make it bulky, the thin supports will give way in the furnace under

[1] The assembler is sometimes called the 'repairer.' The latter term is a little misleading, as it is apt to suggest a man who repairs broken china, rather than one who assembles the parts of a figure.

FIG. 64. WALL-CANDLESTICK
Ludwigsburg; about 1765
Mannheim, C. Baer Collection

the weight. This consideration usually led to the use of the tree-stumps or blocks of stone to be seen in most figures. Their presence would seem quite gratuitous if the reason for them were not known. If we bear in mind that the bottoms of large dishes are always liable to warp in the fire, that the handle of a jug has to be put on crooked so that the fire may correct its position, and that every piece of porcelain contracts during firing by one-sixth of its original volume, we may judge how much forethought and experience are necessary to pilot such wayward children through all the perils of adolescence. In making the clay model it required a fine sense of artistic values to visualize the effect the figure must produce in the quite different medium of porcelain. The play of light on the dazzling white surface of glazed porcelain demanded a totally different style of modelling from the dull matt clay; so that from the first the stresses to be marked in the clay model were quite different from the stresses required if the model were to be reproduced in, say, marble or alabaster.

All these were difficulties of technique and of art, but every factory had also its economic difficulties. Porcelain had to be sold, and therefore the factory must show a profit. The reigning prince wanted revenue as well as entertainment. The middle-class proprietors wanted a positive return on their labours, but it was in fact rare for a factory to bring in a large income. It is true that when Meissen had the monopoly of manufacture in Germany, and had passed the stage of expensive experiments, the factory provided the royal treasury with a handsome revenue. Between 1733 and 1735 the net profits were estimated at about one and a half million thalers (the thaler was equivalent to about 3*s.* pre-War). Again, between 1733 and 1748 Augustus III alone ordered porcelain, for gifts and for his own use, to the value of 516,669 thalers; and large sums were spent on innumerable services and works of art executed without payment to the orders of the director, Count Brühl, and other people in high places. Thus it is scarcely surprising that the number of workmen constantly increased. Four hundred men were employed at Meissen in 1742, and in 1754 their number had risen to 578.

FIG. 65. LARGE WALL-CLOCK
Frankenthal; about 1760
Munich, Bayerisches National-Museum

In the second half of the eighteenth century rival factories sprang up like mushrooms all over Germany, and Meissen again had great difficulties to contend with. Artistically Meissen had remained stationary while other factories had realized the importance of keeping up-to-date; and it

FIG. 66. WATCH-STAND
Nymphenburg; about 1760–65
Munich, Bayerisches National-Museum

always pays to be up-to-date. In 1775 Meissen was working with a deficit of 50,000 thalers, and in 1790 the situation was so critical that the factory asked for a subsidy of 30,000 thalers and a grant of 9000, cut prices heavily so as to inflate the business, sold unpainted porcelain, and even had recourse to lotteries. A not inconsiderable income was provided by the numerous shooting festivals which were held everywhere in the eighteenth century as public entertainments. Some of the prizes were of porcelain, as in 1720 at the Shooting Club in the Favourite Garden at Vienna, where coffee and chocolate sets as well as Tokay services were offered as prizes. Similar things were distributed in the 'lucky dips.' Frederick the Great compelled the lottery clubs to take 6000 thalers' worth of porcelain from his factory every year, and a good

FIG. 67. OIL SET
Nymphenburg; about 1765
Formerly in the Mühsam Collection, Berlin

market for Berlin porcelain was created by a decree of 1769 that all Jews must buy a certain quantity of porcelain (300 thalers on the average) and export it abroad if they sought permission to marry or to purchase real property. The compulsory purchase of 'Jews' porcelain' was first abolished by Frederick William II.

Lotteries and auctions were the last resort of the smaller factories, especially in Thuringia, if the regular demand of the town or the foreign agencies failed to bring in sufficient orders. Moreover, every state possessing its own porcelain factory took steps to protect it from the invasion of foreign porcelain. It was thus a great blow to Meissen when Frederick the Great, who had taken over the Berlin factory from Gotzkowsky in 1763, prohibited the sale of Saxon porcelain in Prussia, and even its transport through Prussian territory; and again when Austria, Denmark, Sweden, and Portugal forbade its importation, while other countries put up a high tariff—Russia

FIG. 68. COOLER FOR WINE-GLASSES
Frankenthal; about 1770
Mannheim, Hermannsdorf Collection

40 per cent. and France, Spain, and England 50–60 per cent. On the other hand, we hear of the Government of Schwarzburg-Rudolstadt, and even the noble Prince himself, writing letter after letter to give permission for the small State factory to hold lotteries and auctions of porcelain in Köthen, Würzburg, Bamberg, Altenburg, Giessen, Eschwege, and Oldenburg, Bernburg, Mülhausen, and Münster. It sounds like comic opera or Ruritanian farce. The schemes rarely succeeded, since the countries concerned had their own ceramic establishments and were frightened of being undersold by their competitors. In the 1770's the Volkstedt factory, like some

other Thuringian factories, adopted the quite dishonest practice of adding its own mark (in this case the fork from the arms of Schwarzburg) to the crossed swords of Meissen, in the hope that they might be confused. It even had the effrontery to offer porcelain marked thus for sale at the Leipzig fair. This was more than the Meissen factory could stand. On the protest of Meissen all the Volkstedt goods were confiscated,

FIG. 69. TRAY
Frankenthal; about 1770
Mannheim, Hermannsdorf Collection

and their sale at the fair and their transport through Saxony were prohibited. Volkstedt was not allowed to sell its porcelain again at the Leipzig fair until the Prince of Schwarzburg-Rudolstadt had interceded personally with the Elector of Saxony, and the tenant of the factory had adopted a humbler tone and a mark not liable to confusion.

An important economic factor in many porcelain works was the export trade to the East, especially Turkey. Here Oriental and German interests first came into collision, and here it was a question of disturbing, and eventually destroying, the ancient commercial relations between Turkey and China.

Meissen herself had taken the offensive. As early as 1732 we hear of an order by a Turkish merchant for 2000 dozen of small cups without handles, *Turkenkopgen* as they were called. Later on other factories (*e.g.*, Nymphenburg) entered the field, and even Thuringia took a lively part in the trade. At Passau and Regensburg, on the Danube, a flourishing industry sprang up, occupied in painting the special types of porcelain made for the Levantine market; and it is scarcely surprising that these porcelains were provided with special marks to delude the unsuspecting Turk that he was buying Chinese goods. In this export trade Meissen again took the lead; apparently it was a request from the Turkish merchant Manasses Athenas that caused the adoption in 1731 of a Mercury's staff as a mark for the Turkish export wares, instead of the more usual crossed swords from the Electoral coat of arms. Imitations of Chinese and Japanese marks occur fairly frequently on Meissen pieces, especially the Turkish wares.

CHAPTER III

VESSELS

1. Coffee and Table Services: Other Useful Wares: Vases

Among the products of a porcelain factory we may distinguish two main classes, vessels and figures, or, if you like, useful and ornamental wares. Both categories had a quite definite place in the culture of the eighteenth century. It was obvious from the beginning that a substance of such rare delicacy was intended for table- and drinking-vessels, for which purpose it had been used in China and had been already copied in European faience. Before Böttger's invention various materials were used for these purposes. The poor man's table had glazed earthenware or pewter, while faience or the precious metals graced the tables of the rich. Now faience and silver found a strong competitor in porcelain, and were more and more confined to well-to-do households. To an increasing extent porcelain was used for all kinds of table ware, for many other objects of daily use, and especially, of course, for the more exacting demands of elegance and luxury.

Breakfast sets and table services were the staple product of all factories. What did these services consist of? Porcelain objects preserved in collections give us an excellent idea of some of the constituent pieces. The descriptions of others are known to us from various price lists of some of the most important factories, notably Meissen and Nymphenburg, which have fortunately been preserved, and give us valuable information of the current wares and their prices. The large 'current price lists' are, however, comparatively late, the Meissen list dating from 1765 and the Nymphenburg list from 1767. But they will suffice for the following remarks, since we cannot attempt here a general economic history of the different factories, and therefore scarcely touch on the large body of similar material published from the documentary records of the other factories.

The Meissen price list of 1765 begins with coffee services, of which no less than eighty-four varieties are enumerated, those with simple decoration being again divided into two sections: "fine quality" and "medium quality." The Nymphenburg list of 1767 is content with nineteen varieties,

FIG. 70. TRAY WITH SCENE PAINTED IN PURPLE
Fulda; about 1770
Mannheim, Hermannsdorf Collection

divided among three classes: "fine quality," "medium quality," and "inferior quality." The latter were not usually sold at Meissen; so also with white unpainted porcelain, which Nymphenburg likewise divided into three classes. The enormous difference in price between the different qualities may be judged from the fact that at Meissen a complete coffee set in a good-quality ware of simple shape, with underglaze painting in blue, cost 19.8 thalers, while at Nymphenburg it cost 35 florins. On the other hand, the most expensive style of service, with Watteau figures painted *en mosaïque*, is priced at 248.18 thalers by Meissen and at 300 florins by Nymphenburg.

All these "complete coffee services" consisted of twelve coffee-cups with handle, six chocolate-cups with handle, slop-basin, coffee-pot, milk-jug, teapot, sugar-basin, tea-caddy, and bread-and-butter plate; at Nymphenburg the latter was called a "bread-plate" (*Brod-Tasse*), which name shows that it was used for white bread. In other factories—*e.g.*, Fürstenberg—it was called a "sweet-meat-dish" (*Zucker-oder Einsatz-Schale*). Besides these things, which were made everywhere in various shapes and sizes, certain other objects were advertised separately. Thus at Meissen we find coffee-cups without handle — *i.e.*, "Turkish cups" (*Turkenkopgen*)—specially made in seventy-three different patterns, also teacups, with or without handle, teaspoon, and 'oak-leaf' (a plate in the form of an oak-leaf). Nymphenburg mentions some further pieces: teacups (*Theeschalen*) with a handle, tea-strainers, a "teapot for sixteen cups [*i.e.*, to hold sixteen cups] with *réchaud* and spirit-lamp," and also sugar-basins (*Zuckertassen*) and milk-jugs (*Milchtöpfgen*) with pointed spout. From the composition of the complete service it is evident that as a rule the coffee-pot was used for chocolate as well as for coffee, and that the coffee-cups were commonly used for tea as well. There are, however, certain differences of shape between teacups and coffee-cups: the teacups have a pronounced bowl shape, shallower than the taller coffee-cups, whereas the chocolate-cups are a steeper

FIG. 71. POT-POURRIER
Fürstenberg; about 1770
Mannheim, Hermannsdorf Collection

and taller shape, approximating a cylinder. But in the composition of all these services one object is lacking which we frequently meet in old porcelain—the tray, or "service-plate" (*Anbiet-Platte*). Its absence is natural enough in large services with a dozen or half a dozen cups, but it invariably accompanies the small services, which were not included in the big price lists, in the eighteenth century colloquially described as *tête-à-tête* and *solitaire* sets. The *tête-à-tête* is a breakfast set, or *déjeuner*, for two persons (Fig. 39), the *solitaire* for one person, there being respectively two cups or one. These small *déjeuner* sets always have their service-plate, a large plate usually oval in shape and with horizontal ear-handles, on which the other vessels are brought in. At the present day we should call it a tea-tray, or server. In these smaller breakfast services the separate pieces often vary in number and style. The slop-basin is wanting, since it would take up too much room on the tray. In other cases, where the user drank only coffee, the tea-caddy is omitted, or replaces the coffee-pot, as in the exquisite Berlin *solitaire* with scenes from Lessing's play *Minna von Barnhelm* (Figs. 90 and 91), which is simply a tea set. Thus the combinations vary according to purpose or individual taste. Another composition for a *déjeuner* is given in the Fürstenberg price list for 1779. It reads thus:

> In the *déjeuner* coffee set are included: one coffee-tray, one coffee-pot, one cream-jug, one sugar-basin, two pairs of coffee-cups with handles, and two spoons. In the *déjeuner* tea set are included: one tea-tray, one teapot, one cream-jug, one sugar-basin, one pair of cups, and one spoon.

Why the two tea-drinkers had to be content with one spoon is a riddle.

A special charm attaches to services where the old leather case has been preserved, with its silk or velvet lining and close-fitting sockets for each piece. Such cases were made chiefly for expensive services and for travellers. We may also mention a special form of cup which has not been noticed in the foregoing survey—the socket-cup, or *trembleuse*, made for the use of a shaky hand (Figs. 37 and 73). In the saucer there is a cylindrical ring of open trellis-work which serves as a socket for the cup and has a nick for the handle, so that when the cup is in position it cannot fall over.

The second great system of useful vessels is the dinner service. Here there is no definite rule for the number of constituent pieces. The plates were, of course, made in sets of a dozen, according as the service was to be used for large or small families, banqueting-tables, and the like. A typical complete dinner service consisted of the following vessels: *hors d'œuvres* plates, soup-plates, several large dishes, salad-bowls, tureens with stands, compotiers, meat-plates, sauce-boats, butter-dishes, butter-boats, salt-cellars, knife-handles, cruet spoons, mustard-spoons, a *plat de ménage* of eleven or six pieces, punch-bowls, with or without cover, punch-ladles, soup-ladles, table-chandeliers, hand-candlesticks, sweetmeat-dishes of various kinds, finger-bowls with ewers, table-jugs, soup-pots with stands, soup-bowls with stands, and broth-pots with stands. Nearly all these things were made in various sizes. To these were added other pieces specified as "for dessert": plates with open-work borders, various sweetmeat-dishes in the form of poplar-leaves, sun-flowers, cabbage-leaves, or vine-

FIG. 72. WARMING-POT
Höchst; about 1770
Frankfort-on-the-Main, Historisches Museum

leaves, open-work sweetmeat-baskets oval and round, and round and oval baskets on four timbered legs.

With certain variations the constitution of the Meissen dinner services is also applicable to Nymphenburg. The large *plats de ménage* specified in the catalogue are missing, and probably were not made there. The high price, which at Meissen ranged from 18 to 90 thalers according to the quality of the painting, suggests that they were pieces of special importance. Such a *plat de ménage* is in fact a regular table-centre. It consisted of a large pedestal with a high superstructure round which were arranged the various jugs or bottles for oil and vinegar, etc., sugar-caster, and cruets for salt, pepper, and other spices. Little baskets supported by figures were sometimes used for salt and pepper. Thus the Meissen price list under the head of figures explicitly mentions "children with baskets for *plat de ménage*" (quoted at 3.4 thalers apiece). At Nymphenburg a tureen is known as a *Potaoile*, or oil-pot, and we also hear of sugar-bowls with cover, salad-bowls (*Salattöpfe*), *Cocot-Gefasse und Töpfgen* (vessels for cream—a Frankenthal price list for 1777 mentions "*Cocots*, or pots for cream," the name being spelt *Coquets* at Fürstenberg), *Cucumer-Tassen* (perhaps for cucumber-juice), *Port-Caraffe* (stands for decanters), *Corvines oder Käntel* (little jugs with small angular lip-spouts like a bird's bill), and wine-bottles. Finally, mention is made of *Alant* (meaning uncertain), *Rossoli-Becher* (small cups which constantly reappear in Bohemian glass of the *Biedermeier* period and were used for a liqueur called Rossoli, made of brandy, sugar, and cinnamon, often with the addition of various perfumes), *Ayr-Einsätze* (egg-cups), and lastly *sceaux*, the latter in three varieties, *pousirt* (*i.e.*, with relief decoration), "with handle," and "oval for liqueur-glasses." These *sceaux* are refrigerators. The "oval *sceaux* for liqueur-glasses" are identical with the peculiar oval tubs with vertical sides and a wavy rim. They are commonly mistaken for *jardinières*, but their function was quite different: they contained iced water in which the glasses (the "liqueur-glasses" of the Nymphenburg catalogue) were suspended with the bowls downward to be chilled (Fig. 68). In the Frankenthal catalogue for 1777, already cited, *sceaux* are called simply "oval or round cooling-buckets for *Stengelgläser*" (tall cylindrical drinking-glasses). In other places—*e.g.*, Vienna—*sceaux* appear to have meant bottle-coolers, coolers for glasses being designated *verriers*. This is evident from the catalogue of a service (part of which still exists at Leningrad)

FIG. 73. COVERED CUP AND SAUCER OF THE TYPE KNOWN AS TREMBLEUSE

Cf. Fig. 37. Fürstenberg; about 1780

Frankfort-on-the-Main, Kunstgewerbemuseum

made at the Vienna factory in 1786 as a gift from the Emperor to Paul, Heir Apparent to the Russian throne. This unusually large service consisted of no less than 659 pieces, to which were added 72 knife-handles and a complete set of table ornaments consisting of biscuit figures in the classical style.

It may be of interest to add that at Frankenthal a complete table service for twelve covers consisted of the following pieces: twelve soup-plates, sixty meat-plates, two oval and two round tureens with stands, two large oval dishes, four of medium size, and eight small ones, two large round dishes, two of medium size, and eight small ones, two large salad-bowls, two sauce-boats with stands, two mustard-pots with spoons, six round fruit-dishes, four salt-cellars, two butter-dishes with stands, and twelve *Cocots*, or cream-pots, making a total of nearly 140 pieces.

Apart from these objects, which made the normal constitution of the table service, the entire equipment of a 'good' table admitted several other things which were not mentioned in the price list. Thus the large and celebrated services made at Meissen for Counts Brühl and Sulkowsky included orange-holders, containers for bunches of grapes, sausage-pot, and vermouth-cup. Berlin was specially fond of warming-dishes, which constantly occur in the royal services and take the place of the chafing-dishes usually made of silver.

These pretty well exhaust the repertory of the porcelain factories so far as services are concerned. In the Meissen price list they are followed by "Various porcelain articles, unclassified," such as "stands for writing-sets" (inkstands), "writing-sets, ink-bottle, and sand-box," quill-holders, hand-bells for writing-sets (Figs. 30 and 31), complete writing-sets of five, six, and even thirteen pieces, chamber-pots, soap-dishes, pomade-pots, a "mounted tea-kettle [*i.e.*, with bronze handle] with open-work pedestal and spirit-lamp" priced at 45 thalers (*cf.* Fig. 36), and lastly four types of stand or case for clocks and watches, richly decorated with figures and painting, and priced at from 40 thalers to 80. Some of these things are omitted from the Nymphenburg catalogue, while others are added: wash-basins and ewers, spittoons and stands, night-lights, censers with cover and stand, spirit-flasks for the latter, holy-water jugs, clock-cases with console, clock-dials, barbers' bowls, pedestals *en quarré*, salt-spoons, coffee-spoons, and *Spiritusfläschgen* (smelling-bottles).

Most factories attached some importance to the production of clocks, some of them quite simple, others overdecorated. As examples we illustrate a Nymphenburg watch-stand by Bustelli in the liveliest rococo style (Fig. 66) and a huge

Frankenthal clock, in the Bayerisches National-Museum, in which the arch of the console contains one of the largest Frankenthal groups (Fig. 65). Plastic work in porcelain was naturally applied to lighting-pieces. The most beautiful Berlin model for a lustre is shown in Fig. 63, while Fig. 64 illustrates a splendidly modelled wall-candlestick with admirable painting of mythological scenes.

To these we add "confinement tureens" (round tureens with covers and stands), since, filled with delicacies, they were a very favourite present in Germany to women during confinement, and are frequently found in pewter, silver, and faience as well as in porcelain. The Vienna price list of services already cited mentions them under the description *petites jattes ou écuelles pour maladies* ("small bowls or basins for ladies who are indisposed"). Mention may be made also of oil sets (*huiliers*), often in very choice designs, as in the Nymphenburg specimen of Fig. 67. A larger number of jugs and bottles produced a kind of *plat de ménage.* The latter often takes peculiar forms. Thus the *plat de ménage* was made in the form of a ship, with the oil- and vinegar-cruets, peppers and salts, mustard-pot, and sugar-caster standing on the deck. Lastly the Nymphenburg list refers to "*pot-pourri* set consisting of two vases, barrel-shaped, two ditto round with cover, one ditto round, one ditto large," and also "vases with cover and three feet." Strangely enough these are the only allusions to vases. The Meissen list does not mention them at all. Nevertheless we know from the great quantities of porcelain surviving that vases were a high percentage of the output of all factories. They were made either singly or in sets of at most five

FIG. 74. COVERED CUP AND SAUCER
Fulda; about 1780
Formerly in the Mühsam Collection, Berlin

pieces simply as ornaments, *garnitures de cheminée*, wall-decorations, and so on; or, again, they served special purposes as pot-pourriers (*Riechtopf*—"perfume-pot"), being so described in the Nymphenburg price list. The use of pot-pourriers persisted well into the nineteenth century. A vase like those mentioned was filled with a mixture of salt with rose-petals and rose-leaves, lavender, and other fragrant flowers, which gave off a soft, pleasant odour. It is impossible to enter here into the numerous styles and shapes of porcelain vases, even though they indicate the stylistic development of European porcelain very clearly and forcibly. The illustrations, however, will give an adequate survey of the development without further commentary.

2. Shaping and Painting of Vessels

(A) *Baroque*

The shapes of all these vessels were derived from Meissen. For thirty years the pioneer factory had no serious competitor in Europe, except Vienna, and it has the credit of creating and defining a series of shapes which, in spite of certain changes of fashion, held the field until the eighth decade of the eighteenth century. Meissen reached this position only after a prolonged course of trial and error. At the beginning there was a natural tendency to adhere too closely to Chinese and Japanese prototypes, amounting at times to mere reproduction, especially in the red Böttger stoneware. But the factory very soon became ambitious to create independent shapes consonant with European taste. Here again there was at first a tendency to borrow, this time from the style of contemporary silver, which was often of angular form decorated in relief with acanthus-leaves and lambrequin patterns (Figs. 19 and 20). We know also that the designs for the stoneware and for the earliest porcelain vessels were executed by an artist in metal, Irminger, the Court Goldsmith at Dresden. Gradually, however, Meissen began to discard these shapes, which were essentially unceramic, and to evolve a vessel style adapted to her material and determined by its peculiar qualities. The shapes are nice and easy, a circular ground-plan being preferred, wherever possible. This shape is,

FIG. 75. POT-POURRIER WITH AN ALLEGORICAL SCENE AND A SILHOUETTE
Berlin; 1785
Mannheim, Hermannsdorf Collection

in fact, the most natural to ceramic art, since the vessel is turned off round when it is thrown on the potter's wheel. Again, very high relief is a contradiction of the nature of porcelain, since the glaze always has a tendency to take the edge off ridges and projections, and to gather in the hollows. From the first the taste for decoration in colours was a strong influence on form, leading to shapes with ample surface. As the control of colour became more accurate and its artistic uses were better understood, there was a corresponding demand for vessels with more surface as a ground for painting. Thus it is far from being an accident that the first classics of form in porcelain appeared during the decade when a painter of genius, J. G. Herold, was art-dictator of the Meissen factory.

We have already said that Herold, after a short stay at the Vienna factory, migrated to Meissen in the year 1720. He was only three-and-twenty when he was appointed director of painting. He brought discipline to a staff which had grown extremely slack under the too brilliant government of Böttger. He improved the colours and introduced important technical innovations in the kilns. Most important of all, he defined the style of the new painting. The rather arid and laborious patterns and calligraphies of the style known as *Laub- und Bandelwerk* ('foliage-and-band work') were now superseded. The use of a rich and luscious palette produced richer and livelier ornament, which, at the King's desire, followed the precedents of China and Japan. The finest works of this period, the large vases designed for the adornment of the Japanese Palace, are usually decorated in one of two distinct styles. The first style has large-scale flower-paintings of extraordinary brilliance, with birds and other creatures, and is derived throughout from Oriental prototypes. The second is the peculiar style consisting of figure subjects and known as *chinoiserie*. It was not actually invented by Herold, but was developed by him to full artistic independence of China. The books of travel mentioned above and their engravings (which as representations of fact are quite untrustworthy), together with the figure-paintings on Chinese porcelain, lacquer, and other things, seized the fancy of European artists. The Chinese style rapidly invaded all departments of decorative art, and designers in France, as well as decorative engravers in Germany, produced *chinoiseries* in large numbers, many of them full of spirit and charm. Herold adorned this style with easy grace and inexhaustible humour. In his engravings, and especially in his paintings, he created fantastic variations on the Chinese theme. For they are not real Chinese, the 'Chinamen' who wander in these strange shrubberies, and drink tea, and practise magic, and do combat with monsters; but a little people, of absurd garments and enormous hats and long

FIG. 76. COVERED CUP AND SAUCER OF THE PATTERN KNOWN AS VASENFÖRMIG MIT STÄBEN ('VASE-SHAPED WITH RIBS')
Berlin; about 1785
Mannheim, Hermannsdorf Collection

mustachios and pigtails, leading an intricate, dreamy sort of life in an amazing landscape inhabited by winged dragons, and birds of incredible shape, and insects of fearful size. Such *chinoiseries* appear in gracefully bordered reserves against grounds of various colours, which are a special glory of Meissen (Fig. 28). Sometimes they run round the cups and jugs and tureens of a service, or they are arranged in small oval or quatrefoil compartments surrounded by an elegant border of cresting in gold, purple, and iron red on a lustrous mother-of-pearl ground (see frontispiece).

Direct Oriental influence is evident in another very large group of early Meissen paintings. With the Chinese porcelain imported during the reign of Augustus the Strong came a considerable quantity of the porcelain known as Imari ware, with which Fig. 11 has already acquainted us. The decoration of these wares covers the ground with an economy of design which gives a specially piquant and delicate effect, and Herold and his painters were greatly attracted by them. The

FIG. 77. CENTRE-PIECE WITH OPEN-WORK DECORATION
Meissen; about 1785
Berlin, Mühsam Collection

fine white surface of the porcelain was here used with splendid effect, and sets off to perfection the sparkling jewellery of enamel colours. One of these designs, which were chiefly employed for useful vessels, is illustrated in Fig. 24. It is known as the 'yellow tiger' pattern, and was reserved for the royal table. The two toilet services in Figs. 22, 23 are painted principally with charming flower designs under the influence of Japanese porcelain. Fig. 29 shows the other side of the vase with sea-green ground illustrated in Fig. 28. Here *chinoiserie* in the style of Herold and a copy of a Japanese figure subject appear in the same piece, an unusual combination (*cf.* the plate in Fig. 11). This vase, with its fellow, is also interesting because it illustrates the division of labour, often considerable, at the Meissen factory. The front, with its *chinoiserie*, is painted, if not by Herold himself, at any rate by one of his best colleagues; the back, with the Japanese design, has been quite recently shown to be the work of A. F.

FIG. 78. COVERED CUP AND SAUCER WITH SILHOUETTE OF COUNTESS MARCOLINI
Meissen; about 1790
Mannheim, Hermannsdorf Collection

von Löwenfinck, who has been already mentioned. It is also certain that the green ground was done by a third painter, and probably a fourth was responsible for the flowers in the white border at the bottom. We may probably assume that a fifth hand executed the gilt decoration, and it is certain that the large *AR* mark (for *Augustus Rex*) in underglaze blue was done by a special blue-painter.

Vases naturally show the influence of the strong or graceful, but always superb, shapes of K'ang Hsi porcelain; they show too a new idiom in the making. Under Herold the shapes of vessels, especially jugs, discovered a classic form which showed few alterations and improvements in the succeeding period. But in the year 1731 there entered the Meissen factory an artist who was destined to set the history not only of Meissen, but of European porcelain as a whole. This was the statuary Johann Joachim Kändler. As a young man he had been nursed in the thundering baroque style which had made Dresden one of its grandest conquests, and he now passed on the same baroque accent to all productions of the porcelain factory. Of his figure models we shall speak later. After he took on the 'white gang' the vases and other vessels assumed, for the most part, an entirely new character. In the shapes of vessels there suddenly appears a new life and rhythm; profiles acquire power and movement, surfaces become volumes, the feet of tureens turn off into scrolls, the handles have an elastic energy. Everywhere style followed the lead of a born modeller, who forced his material to its utmost capacity for form; indeed, from the point of view of abstract æsthetics, he scarcely stopped at violation. His irrepressible impulse to form is strikingly expressed in two luxury services of world-wide renown which were made entirely in porcelain: the Swan service, modelled during the years 1737–41 for Count Brühl, and a service made a little earlier for Count Sulkowsky. A characteristic feature in the Swan service is the striving for plastic expression on every inch of available surface, so that little remains for the painter but minor embellishments, apart from the elaborate gilding which stresses the powerful rhythm of each piece. The other painting consists entirely of scattered 'Indian blooms' (flowers in the Japanese Imari style), the Count's quarterings, and a limited amount of ornament on the elaborate figure-mouldings. The tureen illustrated in Fig. 32 belongs to about the same period as the two services mentioned. The splendid form of this piece, its lively profile, and every detail of its modelling declare it to be Kändler's work, dating from the decade 1730–40, when the artist was in full enjoyment of his creative power and had carried the Meissen factory with him to the zenith of its achievement.

This, the most brilliant, period of Meissen porcelain was

dominated throughout by a rich and ponderous baroque. Then the tide turned. The enormous long wigs grew shorter. Among the swelling curves and scrolls of the style to which the French *Roi Soleil* (Louis XIV) has given his name, playful and petulant little flourishes appeared. A new idea of life, gay and gracious, superseded the formality and solid worth of earlier days. *Andante maestoso* gave way to *allegretto*. The rococo had set in.

The one factory which stood with Meissen during the early baroque period was that of Vienna. It is worth remark that

FIG. 79. BREAKFAST SET WITH VIEWS OF MUNICH
Painted by P. Böhngen. Nymphenburg; about 1815
Munich, Bayerisches National-Museum

both in the form and in the decoration of vessels Vienna at this time went all her own way. Meissen influence can scarcely be traced. During the first period, under du Paquier (1718–44), Vienna produced very little work in detached figures, but her vessels were freely embellished with plastic ornament in the form of the popular Callot figures and other caricatures. Other moulded extras, such as zoomorphic handles, were also introduced, usually on purely baroque shapes, which can be derived from contemporary silver as certainly as the earliest Meissen vessels. Vienna, too, had first to discover her own idiom in ceramic art. But in the parts of services Vienna never went so far as did Kändler in the Swan service, where even the surfaces of plates are overgrown with a rich relief decoration of swans and other creatures. Vienna always had more restraint, and in her vessels and vases kept as far as possible to plain surfaces. In decoration the painter held the place of honour, and even in the painting we may notice a great contrast to Meissen. The wide range

FIG. 80. VASE WITH SCENES FROM THE ITALIAN TRAVELS OF THE CROWN PRINCE LUDWIG IN 1817
Nymphenburg (after Georg Dillis); 1821
Munich, Bayerisches National-Museum

of style in Meissen painting is not to be found at Vienna; there is indeed no lack of attractive *chinoiseries* and due borrowing of other Oriental themes, but the main body of Vienna painting from 1720 to 1740 follows the style known as *Laub- und Bandelwerk*, in which the entire vessel is covered with a system of strong calligraphic ornament and lambrequin motives (mainly in purple, iron red, and gold), obviously suggested by the Augsburg pattern books. This convention is typical of Vienna, as it is a rare phenomenon at Meissen, except during the early period. The borders of *Laub- und Bandelwerk* which frame the panel-paintings of Meissen are delightfully spirited paraphrases, and quite a distinct type. On the other hand, the flower-paintings known as *deutsche Blumen* appear at Vienna very early (about 1725), and from Vienna seem to have been adopted at a later date by Meissen.

(B) *Rococo*

The transference of the Vienna factory to the State in 1744 marks the second stage in the history of its art, naturally dominated by the rococo style. The same thing happened at Meissen. As early as 1730 *rocaille* forms, little flourishes, and broken volutes shyly began to declare themselves, and gradually superseded the heavy forms of baroque. Then the transition became fairly rapid, and towards 1740 the rococo style, guided by the two masters Kändler and Herold, had been victorious all along the line.

The new vessel forms which now appeared are a good index of the change in taste. If we leave on one side the plain plate forms ultimately derived from China, a moulded border with a pattern resembling basket-work, the so-called *Ordinair-Ozier*, or 'ozier pattern,' was already used in the 1730's, and in the 'Brandenstein variants' (*Brandenstein-Variante*) zig-zag ribs were allowed to intrude on to the clear surface. Hitherto the principle had always been to keep the centre of the plate smooth, as a ground for painting, and it was, of course, more consistent with the function of the plate. But during the 1740's new patterns were devised in which the distinction between rim and centre was frequently lost sight of, and the rim patterns of *rocaille* work, flower-sprays and the like, straggled over the middle of the plate. This tendency is fully accounted for by a fear of hard-and-fast divisions which was in the nature of rococo. A gentle mingling and meandering of form was now cultivated deliberately, on the same principle that the stucco decoration of rococo ceilings finds its way beyond the limits of the vault and down on to the walls. In the actual ornament there appears the new principle of asymmetry, waywardness, a graceful formlessness; and, in fact, no material is better suited than porcelain to decoration thus free from stiffness and restraint. The pretty scrolls and light bouquets in their low

FIG. 81. PLATE WITH VIRGINS ADORNING A FIGURE
Vienna; about 1800
Frankfort-on-the-Main, Kunstgewerbemuseum

relief, with the gay colour of the enamels on the shining white glaze, are charmingly effective. In the larger pieces, in tureens, jugs, and the like, a certain irregularity of form is of practical value, since the pieces were all too apt to warp in the fire; and when the outlines were clean and the surfaces unbroken, the effect of this would naturally be more noticeable. The handles and snouts of jugs are especially characteristic of the change in style. At an earlier date the handles had been rounded in fat contented curves like an S, but they now acquire a lively abandon and a certain tense energy, while their rhythm is arrested and rambles off into flourishes. Scrolls in relief give the snouts a restless, excited outline, and the knob of the cover, previously of graceful baluster or bullet form, is now replaced by a fruit or rose-bud.

With the triumph of the rococo style the painting assumed quite a different character. Towards the end of the decade 1730–40 *chinoiseries* dropped into the background. Their place was taken by various European themes, among which landscapes with more or less elaborate accessories, and groups of figures in the style of Watteau, play the leading part. The passion for hunting in the Court society of the day is reflected in finely painted hunting scenes, while hand-to-hand fighting is represented in battle scenes. Harbour pictures, with ships and merchandise in the foreground, were also great favourites; river landscapes are frequent, and often show views of the Saxon Switzerland (the Königstein) and the environs of Dresden. Last but not least, *fêtes champêtres*, romantic rural entertainments of the aristocracy and the gentry, were painted on *déjeuners*, *solitaires*, and other porcelain delights, in charming miniature and in all the varieties of a lively fancy. Such subjects were either enclosed in medallions reserved in coloured grounds, or painted on the white surface of the porcelain and surrounded by beautiful and often very elaborate borders of cresting. It must not be supposed, however, that all these colour-painters of the Meissen

FIG. 82. TEAPOT
Venice; about 1725
Hamburg, Tillmann Collection

factory were original artists. The subjects of their painting were almost always taken from engravings which reproduced on a small scale the great works of the most important con-

FIG. 83. SÈVRES VASE WITH BLUE GROUND (BRONZE MOUNTS)
Paris, private collection

temporary painters. Through the medium of these copper-plates, paintings on porcelain were sponsored by Watteau, Lancret, Pater, and other masters of the day. But that is a question of the sources of design, and must be left to a later context.

We have now to deal with an entirely new flora. The

stylized Oriental, or 'Indian,' flowers were becoming old-fashioned, and were now confined to the flowered patterns of figure costume. They were superseded during the decade

FIG. 84. SÈVRES VASE WITH ROSE-COLOURED GROUND
Paris, private collection

1740–50 by 'German' flowers, the flora of German fields and gardens: roses, forget-me-nots, carnations, narcissi, pansies, singly in broadcast, and loosely tied in posies, in single colours such as purple, blue, iron red, green, or in a brilliant variety of enamel colours. In the early stages this flower-painting was dependent on engraved prototypes, and followed a lifeless linear style, often with strong hatched shadows, as in the service made for Clement Augustus, Elector of Cologne (Fig. 33). Insects and scattered sprigs of flowers were used to enliven the white surface, and especially to cover flaws in the glaze. From about the middle of the eighteenth century the process went further, and the flowers were copied direct from nature in a light, flossy, very agreeable style in which the natural colours of the various flowers were rendered as closely as possible. This had never been the case when the paintings were taken from engravings. The new fashion in flower-painting received the name 'natural flowers.' Then there appeared garlands, still-life fruit, birds, poultry, cattle, peasant scenes—to mention only the most important. And where the rim is no longer decorated and enlivened with a design in relief it is painted with a wide 'mosaic' of scale or trellis pattern in strong colours, divided from the painted subject proper by an irregular dentil border in gold or colours.

The foregoing account has been confined to the vessels of Meissen. But after the middle of the eighteenth century Meissen encountered formidable competition from other factories which were now springing up in quick succession. It is true that the standards established by the great Meissen factory were still unassailed, but other factories had created their own idioms in vessel style, and in that department were producing works of great distinction both in form and painting. Chief among them was Berlin, whose vessels are her special glory. During her rococo period she employed no plastic artists of real note, but in the delicate beauty and rich colouring of her painted services she is without question ahead of all other German factories. A determining influence on the artistic output of the factory and its peculiar style was the strong interest taken in it by Frederick the Great. He had a passion for the lovely stuff, and during the Second Silesian War (1745) when Meissen was occupied by the Prussians he took away porcelain to the value of 100,000 thalers. During the Seven Years War again considerable quantities of porcelain were seized, but Meissen also executed large orders of the King which were paid for, among them six large

FIG. 85. TEA SERVICE PAINTED BY TAILLANDIER
Sèvres; 1777
Hamburg, Museum für Kunst und Gewerbe

table services. Several Prussian generals of the time knew how to get porcelain 'cheap' at Meissen. We learn that General Zieten ordered a table service worth 1800 thalers and never paid for it, but gave out that "it might well be a present in return for a successful command."

When Frederick the Great took over the Gotzkowsky factory at Berlin in 1763 he maintained a constant and active connexion with the business, keeping a critical eye on the workmen and giving large orders, mainly for comprehensive table services for the various palaces. The years immediately preceding 1770 produced, at first under the influence of the Meissen service patterns—*e.g.*, *Ozier* and *Brandenstein* in several varieties—a whole series of fine new designs, including the 'radial design' (*radierte Dessin*) already brought out by Gotzkowsky, which was later called 'relief ornament' (*Reliefzierat*), and in its two varieties 'with ribs' and 'with trelliswork' remained the most popular and beautiful pattern at Berlin. In the years 1763 and 1767 it was followed by the 'new ornament' (*Neuzierat*) and the 'antique ornament' (*Antikzierat*), together with the 'new smooth pattern' (*neuglattes Muster*) and the 'smooth royal pattern' (*königsglattes Muster*) and a model 'vase-shaped with ribs' (*vasenförmig mit Stäben*), which was further developed later under the name 'antique patterns' (*antique Zierathen*) and is known as *Curländer Service* (Fig. 76). It is impossible to give here an exact description of the various patterns; they are adequately discussed in the general literature of porcelain. It need only be remarked that Berlin vessels of the rococo period attained a superb harmony of plastic form, with its rhythm of profile and volume, and painted decoration, which far surpassed the work of any other factory. The services ordered for the New Palace (1765), the Breslau Palace (1767), and the Potsdam Palace (1770), having taken in each case about two years to complete, show the corresponding stages in the artistic development of flower-painting at Berlin (Fig. 38). First there are pale, delicate, casual flowers; then strong colours, and among them the pride of the Berlin factory, a sumptuous, brilliant purple ('rose's anger'); fat, heavy flowers in free co-ordination; and, finally, faithful transcripts of nature with a preference for the more elegant blooms. All these flowers, in the form of bouquets or festoons, combined with wide rim-panels in orange red, blue, or lemon yellow and enriched with gilt *rocaille* in

FIG. 86. REFRIGERATOR FROM THE FLORA DANICA SERVICE
Copenhagen; end of the eighteenth century
Hamburg, Museum für Kunst und Gewerbe

relief, make a wonderful symphony, which has rarely if ever been surpassed (Plate facing p. 62). Berlin now produced a whole series of service types with flower-painting, and at the same time great variety of services with monochrome or two-colour flowers, also in the 'Indian' style, as well as services with classical scenes, bird-paintings (Fig. 39), scenes after Watteau, figures after Teniers, and so on. Very attractive is the *solitaire* with scenes from *Minna von Barnhelm* after engravings by Chodowiecki, which, according to notes in his diary, the artist himself saw made in 1771. It is beyond the scope of this book to enumerate and describe in detail all the different shapes, and the various themes in painting, produced by Meissen and Berlin during the rococo period. The preceding summary and the illustrations may suffice. Nor can we enter here into the peculiarities of the other factories, which all began with *rocaille* forms and *rocaille* painting, and then in the 1770's followed the general tendency of form into the Louis-Seize style. They were influenced throughout by the products of the great pioneer factory at Meissen, although some of them —*e.g.*, Fürstenberg and Ansbach—often conformed to Berlin patterns. But almost all the factories discovered and developed an idiom which distinguishes each of them from the rest, and usually makes it possible for a trained eye to determine the factory at a glance. The shapes of the vessels show their own peculiarities, just as the colours have their distinctive shade. The scheme of colours was differently treated in every factory, and so also was the flower-painting. The landscapes show marked differences of colour and composition, and in every studio the figure-painting favoured a distinct *genre*. Thus we find an infinity of types and specialities which, surveyed as a whole, give an idea of the endless charm and variety of porcelain vessels during the rococo period. But, as I have said already, I cannot enter here into particulars, and must be content to indicate the general type to which they belong. For some of the varieties of form reference may be made to the illustrations of vessels made in other factories which followed the precedents of Meissen and Berlin.

(C) *The Classical Revival*

The multitude of shapes which may be allotted to the rococo period diminishes as we near the end of the eighteenth century. In the 1770's the new classical elements, which had already been developing for some time during the reign of Louis XV, carried everything before them, and brought into fashion the style known as Louis Seize. The transition is often

POLISH GENTLEMAN KISSING A LADY'S HAND

By J. J. Kändler. Meissen; about 1735–40

Munich, Bayerisches National-Museum

difficult to define: the 'antique' had declared itself here and there among the leading factories some time earlier, but side by side with it the popular forms of pure rococo continued in vogue until the 1780's, especially in the smaller factories. Next, some accessories were sacrificed to the new idea of form: the rambling handles of jugs and cups were made rectangular, or in the form of two interlacing staves curved like an ear; the spouts assumed a rectilinear form and an unbroken surface, instead of the rambling shapes decorated with *rocaille* scrolls. Symmetrical fir-cones replace the recumbent rose-buds which had been the characteristic cover knobs of the rococo period. Gradually the actual shapes of vessels followed suit. The oval tray, with its lively scalloped rim and *rocaille* handles, becomes rectangular, octagonal, or circular, with a plain vertical rim; and plates and other vessels lose their pretty relief scrolls. Where relief ornament is still preferred it takes the form of laurel festoons and pendent draperies (Fig. 77). The gentle elastic rhythm of pear-shaped jugs is faulted horizontally by shoulders, and the foot takes a strongly architectural form. Jugs were frequently superimposed on three slanting feet in the form of fluted columns or lion's claws. Finally the jug becomes a truncated cone, and so does the cup. The walls of the saucer, which hitherto were nicely rounded, now take off at an obtuse angle, while vases acquire a square base with meanders in relief and lines of beading (Figs. 79, 80).

The transition from rococo to Louis Seize is certainly illustrated best by the shapes of Sèvres porcelain. Sèvres never went in for the rich relief decoration which we find on German vessels of the decade 1750–60. Her shapes were always plain and simple, to allow as much room as possible for her sumptuous grounds and her brilliant enamel colours; but there was the further technical reason that an easily fusing soft-paste was quite unsuited to sharp relief. Thus did Sèvres make a virtue of necessity.

During the classical period as the shapes changed the painting changed with them. The Watteau scenes now begin to disappear, as we might expect. Harbour scenes and hunting scenes also disappear. The chief survivor is flower-painting, but the bouquets and broadcast flowers have lost their natural vitality and charm. We are in a world of botanical science. The flowers are as dead as a museum. The last word in scientific exactitude appears in the Flora Danica service of the Copenhagen factory, of which one piece (a *glacière*, or refrigerator) is illustrated in Fig. 86. All the pieces in this service bear flowers copied from the *Flora Danica*, an encyclopædia of botany which gives exact representations of all plants native to Denmark. On the bottom of each vessel appear the Latin names of the plants in question, in our case *Potentilla aurea*, *Potentilla anserina*, and (on the fitting) *Conferva hypnoides*.

In another style of flower-painting, popular towards the end of the eighteenth century, especially at Berlin, the flowers are allowed to grow up from the lower rim of cups and jugs as if out of the soil. The stems and plants on either side, mingled with grasses, are arranged in similar fashion, so as to cover the entire cylinder of the vessel. During the Empire and *Biedermeier* periods the flowers had special functions. They were used symbolically to represent a signature—for example, if the name was Carolina you 'said it with flowers' by a garland of Clematis, Anemone, Rose, Oleander, Lily, Iris, Narcissus, and Auricula, the name being concealed in the initials of the flowers. And on innumerable cups of this late period we find a pretty rebus "Change to roses and forget me not," where the roses and forget-me-not are painted 'like life' between the written words. Such things breathe the spirit of the genteel lower-middle-class doggerel of the last century.

In the arid scientific style of flower-painting we may observe a certain pedantry and poverty of fancy, a preoccupation with mere fact, which is also evident in other varieties of porcelain-painting of the Louis-Seize and Empire periods. As a rule the landscapes are no longer imaginary landscapes, but real 'views' of Dresden, Pillnitz, Potsdam, Riddagshausen in Brunswick, Munich, and Mödling, painted with geographical precision (Fig. 79). Much space is also occupied by portraits. These appear in the form of miniature paintings or, more frequently, black silhouettes on cups and saucers, jugs, sugar-basins, and trays, and make a pretty souvenir of individuals, married couples, or entire families (Fig. 78). We may observe here a marked change in the relations between the factory and its circle of customers. Previously these direct orders with definite personal allusions were comparatively rare. They now become more frequent every year. They are nearly

FIG. 87. PART OF A BREAKFAST SET (DÉJEUNER)
Höchst: about 1775–80
Frankfort-on-the-Main, Kunstgewerbemuseum

always found on coffee-cups and other coffee things. The reason is probably that the practice of drinking coffee was becoming increasingly common among the middle classes, and that these cups for personal use were freely given as presents on birthdays and similar occasions. We may suspect, however, that actually they were seldom used. They are rather harmless ornaments for the dresser or the china-cabinet, which becomes fuller and fuller of these sentimental keepsakes as we get nearer to the middle of the nineteenth century.

From the 1780's onwards antiquity won its way into the painting. The recently discovered frescoes at Pompeii, ancient portraits of the Roman emperors, and slavish copies of ancient vase-paintings were freely reproduced. At the same time the shapes of ancient vases and jugs were imitated, and the ear-shaped handles of 'Etruscan' pots were added to the general repertory of form.

A recrudescence of subjects proper to rococo was another peculiarity of the revivalist movement, and is a good indication of the romantic feeling which was the mainspring of the classical style. Even the *chinoiseries*, which at Meissen had disappeared from vessel-painting with the triumph of the rococo style, now reappeared—*e.g.*, at Vienna—mostly in the imitation of Japanese lacquer. On the whole Vienna was the leader of taste among the German factories. The versatility of the Vienna painters is quite astonishing. They could sit any horse; and their use of coloured grounds, their charming schemes of polychrome decoration, and their splendid mastery of gilt relief all have real distinction (Fig. 81). Indeed, they often went too far: frequently the white ground of the porcelain has entirely disappeared. This was, of course, a crime against so beautiful a material, but a crime aggravated by Sèvres, and especially by the smaller French factories of the first half of the nineteenth century. In this over-decorated porcelain the function of the vessels is scarcely evident. All such plates and cups must have been made simply as *bric-à-brac*, more for delight than for use.

3. Sources of Design in Porcelain-painting

We have already mentioned several times the question of the sources or originals of the paintings. It is certain that the more eminent painters were original designers, as Herold at Meissen. But we know that even Herold executed his designs for the use and wont of his painting room, and repeatedly reproduced them by engraving. In whole or part they were to serve as models for the other painters—for in 1731 there were six other painters employed for 'Japanese figures.' And just as decorative art in general, from the sixteenth century onwards, cannot be thought apart from the standards created by engraved ornament, so the whole of Meissen porcelain-painting of the eighteenth century is in the highest degree dependent on similar engraved precedents. The use of such engravings, of course, took numerous forms. Either they served simply as a stimulus and suggested a general idea, or certain parts were borrowed and assimilated to original work;

FIGS. 88, 89. TWO OF CHODOWIECKI'S ENGRAVINGS FOR LESSING'S PLAY "MINNA VON BARNHELM"
1769

or, again, the whole engraving was copied fairly closely. Modern research has more than once tackled this problem, though never in a systematic fashion; and examples are daily accumulating which strikingly attest the dependence.

Large numbers of the early Meissen shapes were derived from goldsmiths' work; a tureen in the Kändler-Sulkowsky service of 1735 has now been identified as a direct copy of a tureen of Augsburg silver in the Royal Silver Repository at Dresden; and even the early decorative painting of the Böttger period can now be affiliated to earlier engravings in the *Laub- und Bandelwerk* style of contemporary fashion, most of them executed by Augsburg and Nuremberg engravers. We have noticed above the decisive influence of Chinese and Japanese porcelain on the painted ornament of Meissen products in the third and fourth decades of the eighteenth century. Simultaneously appeared the great Herold, with his own *chinoiserie*, influenced by the illustrated books of 'East Indian' travel. Then there were the Watteau paintings, in which individual groups and figures nearly always derive from reproductions of the painter's works by French engravers. No one has yet identified the sources of the river scenes and harbour scenes, but we have no doubt that they will be discovered some day, since the cavalry actions and other battle scenes can be referred to engravings after Rugendas, Wouwerman, and other specialists of the same *genre*. It does not follow that every painting on porcelain was derived from an engraving; naturally among the painters there were always independent spirits, who did original compositions of their own genius. But as a rule the painters, in figure subjects at any rate, relied on one model or another, taking over particular details, or recomposing parts of different engravings, and often producing a spirited version, or adaptation, of the original theme. Not least among items in the archives of the various factories are the bills or receipts for the purchase of engravings. For example, we find that in 1741 Meissen received 230 copper-engravings through Count Brühl's secretary, and that several years later a Paris agent was paid 300 thalers for pictures and engravings. Over a thousand engravings are listed in an *Inventory of the Copper-engravings in the Possession of the Royal Manufactory of True Porcelain at Fürstenberg*, which was compiled in 1770. They are well arranged under the headings of landscapes (including Berchem, Hertel, Weirotter, Waterloo, Zuccarelli, Gessner, Weitsch, Ridinger), figure pieces (Nilson, Hertel, Boucher, Coypel, Eisen, Rubens, Wille, Gravelot, Pillement, Huquier, and others), and flower pieces (Tessier and Vauquier). At Schwarzburg Prince John Frederick on several occasions sends copper-engravings to the Volkstedt factory. In a letter of December 10, 1765, he gives instruc-

FIG. 90. SOLITAIRE WITH PAINTING AFTER CHODOWIECKI

Cf. Figs. 88, 89. Berlin; 1771

Hamburg, Museum für Kunst und Gewerbe

tions for "two broth-pots to be painted with the engravings sent herewith," with the remark "the painter can add something of his own invention as he may think fit." Prince Frederick William Eugene von Hildburghausen kept his factory at Kloster-Veilsdorf constantly supplied with engravings of ornament by French and Augsburg designers. When the Elector Charles Theodore took over the Frankenthal factory the copper-engravings on the premises were valued at 780 florins. In the Berlin factory large numbers of old engravings have been preserved until the present day. The Kupferstichkabinett at Stuttgart now possesses the great collection of prototype engravings used by the Ludwigsburg factory, where Nilson occurs most frequently of all French engravers; and the works formerly used by the Vienna factory are now preserved in the Österreichisches Museum für Kunst und Industrie, at Vienna. It is worth noting that among them are several works of the seventeenth century; but the majority date from the time of the classical revival, including the ornament designs of Albertolli and Cipriani, as well as the great album of Percier and Fontaine.

The sources of many paintings on porcelain have been established by special research or by accidental discoveries. We can cite only a few examples, and those mainly for the purpose of illustrating the procedure of the painters. We have already mentioned the charming Berlin *solitaire* with scenes from Lessing's *Minna von Barnhelm* (Figs. 90, 91). The engravings were executed by Chodowiecki in 1769 (Figs. 88, 89), and in 1771 he saw the service being made in the factory. We may observe how closely the painter followed the treatment of the figures in his model, but entirely reorganized the scene as a whole, moving the situations from the interiors of Lessing's text and Chodowiecki's engravings into the open air. This was quite appropriate, since otherwise he would have been obliged to fit his scenes into a definite frame, as Chodowiecki had done. Enclosure of this kind contradicted the painter's fine sense of his medium. He appreciated the splendid effect to be obtained by the easy, almost imperceptible dwindling of the painted area into the white sheen of the

FIG. 91. TRAY BELONGING TO THE SOLITAIRE IN FIG. 90
Cf. Chodowiecki's engravings in Figs. 88, 89. Berlin; 1771
Hamburg, Museum für Kunst und Gewerbe

bare porcelain ground. So he stuck to the time-honoured practice of rococo, allowing the foreground to die away in little tufts of green and brown grass; and getting rid of the dreary expanse of wall surface, he defined his area by the windy folds of a tent flanked by branches of foliage. The change of style at this period cannot be better illustrated than

FIG. 92. TRAY WITH A SCENE AFTER NILSON
Frankenthal; about 1765
Hamburg, Museum für Kunst und Gewerbe

by a comparison of this painting with the painting of the Höchst *tête-à-tête* in Fig. 87, which was also produced during the decade 1770–80, but in the latter half of it. Here we see how the painter encloses his subjects in an oval panel, and surrounds them with a special border of crossed sprays. And for the Louis-Seize period the frame is sacrosanct.

The waywardness and abandon of rococo painting were now taboo; similarly the petulant rambling borders and feet

FIG. 93. J. E. NILSON'S "REJOICINGS IN PEACE TIME"
Cf. Fig. 92

of rococo chairs now gave place to a firm, plain frame and stable, even feet. The Höchst service is painted with scenes from Monsigny's opera *Rose et Colas*, certainly after contemporary engravings, although they have not been identified. This piece was first produced at the Italian Opera in Paris in 1764, and was revived at Frankfort on several occasions between 1773 and 1780. Goethe saw it there, and in *Dichtung und Wahrheit* remarks on the "very delightful impression" it had left on him, adding: "Even now I can remember those beribboned lads and girls and their movements."

These "beribboned lads and girls" appear again in the painting of the Frankenthal tray in Fig. 92. We also illustrate its prototype (Fig. 93), an engraving by Nilson with the title *Freude in Friedenzeit* (*Rejoicings in Peace Time*). Here the painter has treated his prototype in the same way that the Berlin painter treated the Chodowiecki originals; the background is entirely altered, and the buildings are replaced by a tent with flag flying. The reason is again easy to see: the painter had to reduce an upright composition to diagonal composition. The painter was again in conflict with the engraver, Nilson, over the lateral boundaries of the engraving and the *rocaille* work which fences the foreground; and of these he has given a lighter and looser version.

Lastly, we may compare with its original a Nymphenburg coffee-pot painted with birds (Figs. 94, 95). Here the painter has followed the engraver very closely, for the latter was in the business himself, and worked for the porcelain-painter with a full understanding of his requirements. The author and designer of the *Sammlung von Federvieh, besonders Hausgeflügel* (*Collection of Fowl, especially Poultry*) was Gottlieb Friedrich Riedel, of Ludwigsburg, one of the nomad porcelain-painters. He was born at Dresden in 1724, worked at Meissen from 1743 to 1756, and after a shorter stay at Höchst and Frankenthal was appointed head painter at Ludwigsburg in 1759. Eventually, in 1779, he went to Augsburg as a copper-engraver, and died there in 1784.

Such instances of the use of engravings by porcelain-painters may be quoted by the hundred, but the examples we

FIG. 94. NYMPHENBURG COFFEE-POT WITH BIRD-PAINTING AFTER G. F. RIEDEL

Cf. Fig. 95

Hamburg, Museum für Kunst und Gewerbe

have cited will serve to illustrate the importance of engraving in the painting room of an eighteenth-century factory. Besides

FIG. 95. ENGRAVING BY G. F. RIEDEL
Ludwigsburg. Original of Fig. 94

copper-engravings, to which we may add English mezzotints and coloured engravings of the late eighteenth century, oil-paintings of the same period were frequently used for direct copying. This was a favourite practice at Vienna, where pictures from the imperial collection, as well as the great picture galleries of Czernin, Lamberg, Liechtenstein, and others, were copied by the best painters, such as Daffinger and Herr, on the centres of luxury plates with magnificent rims.

4. Toys and Gadgets

The small trinkets sometimes known as 'gallantries' are a minor phase of eighteenth-century culture, but not without their significance. No material is more suitable than porcelain for pretty *objets de vitrine*, for equipping the work-tables and toilet-tables of ladies of fashion, or for the use of the complete gentleman. And so we find that these objects of 'gallantry' were used for a variety of purposes which are no longer known to us to-day, but had their definite place in the culture of that gallant age. The best known are the little boxes, especially tobacco-boxes. The Meissen price list of 1765 quotes no less than eleven varieties of *Tabattieren*, all of them to be had in three different sizes. The simplest were painted with flowers, both outside and inside; "without mosaic"—that is, without coloured borders of scale pattern—they cost from 6 thalers to 9 according to size; "with mosaic" the price was 8 to 11 thalers. Then come in order of price: flower-painting inside and outside; flowers inside, garlands outside; figures and landscapes inside the lid, with flowers outside (Fig. 96). Further varieties, at prices from 34 to 40 thalers, have figures and landscapes on the inside, while outside there are fruits or garlands, landscapes or figures, "Wouwermans" (scenes after pictures by Wouwerman) or "views," or "Ovid figures." The most expensive kind has "miniature histories" on the inside, figures or views on the outside, and costs between 76 and 88 thalers. But all these were ordinary lines always in stock. In quite a different class are the tobacco-boxes made for royal gifts and decorated inside the lid with miniature portraits of ruling princes. Tobacco-boxes were regarded as great luxuries in the eighteenth century. We know that the French Court gave away tobacco-boxes worth fabulous sums, of the finest goldsmiths' work decorated with enamel and precious stones, as presents to ambassadors and other high officials. This was a form of payment. And, as every schoolboy knows, Frederick the Great had a passion for expensive tobacco-boxes: witness the great collection of boxes now in the Hohenzollern Museum. In actual monetary value the porcelain boxes cannot compare, of course, with these magnificent objects; they were suited rather for private and friendly gifts, the more so because the painted decoration could easily be adapted to every occasion. These portraits occur very frequently, always on the inside of the lid, where they can only be seen when the boxes are opened (Fig. 97). Often first-rate works of art, these portraits rival the works of the best enamel-painters of the time. The boxes were also embellished with coats of arms, mottoes, dedications, subjects intended for special occasions, and, of course, scenes of gallantry, often tending to obscenity. As appears from the price list, the paintings on the outside were usually impersonal. As a rule all four sides, the lid, and the bottom were painted, and they were often adorned with charming *rocaille* and flowers in relief, at any rate on the rims, and to serve as a frame for the picture. Great value was attached to mounts of gilt copper,

FIG. 96. BOX
Meissen; about 1750
Mannheim, C. Baer Collection

silver, or gold. The usual shape is that of a small oblong chest with slightly rounded corners, domed lid, and sides inclined to curvature. We also find round and oval boxes of larger size with two lids and a false bottom. The purpose of these variants is not quite clear. The round and oval kinds may have served for *mouches*, or patches. The use of these things can be traced back to the seventeenth century, but their piquancy was especially appreciated by ladies of the rococo period.

FIG. 97. BOX
Meissen; about 1750
Mannheim, C. Baer Collection

The Nymphenburg price list of 1767 mentions plain oval tobacco-boxes *pour femes et à chasse*, tobacco-boxes with moulding *en quarré à chasse*, and, again, tobacco-boxes "oval or *en quarré*, plain or moulded *pour hommes*"—all at the one price of 5 florins for the best kinds, with flowers in colours, landscapes, and gold rims. Unfortunately the price and other details afford no means of distinguishing which varieties were for ladies' use and which were for gentlemen. Why tobacco-boxes were specially described as *à chasse* remains a puzzle, since the expression cannot here refer intelligibly to *châsse*, meaning 'mounts.' Lastly, Nymphenburg advertised tobacco-boxes with portraits and landscapes at a price varying from 10 to 50 florins. This sum, which would probably secure one of the best painted coffee services, shows what skill and patience were expended on the finest portrait-boxes.

The porcelain factories also made utensils for smokers, as distinct from snuff-takers. First of all comes the pipe-bowl, known in the eighteenth century as *Tabakskopf*, or 'tobacco-

FIG. 98. CANE-HEADS
Modelled by F. A. Bustelli. Nymphenburg; about 1760
Munich, Bayerisches National-Museum

head.' We have seen examples of the rococo period with delightful modelling and painting. They are mentioned at Meissen in 1765, plain or with ornament, painted with natural flowers; or they had a girl's head, or were in the form of a Pole or a hussar, a Bacchus or a Turk. The price varied from 12 groschen to 1 thaler, 8 groschen. Nymphenburg offered only three kinds: *pousirt und mit Gesicht* ("moulded and with mask"), *mit Schäfergesicht* ("with shepherd mask"), and *Türkengesicht* ("Turk mask").

Of all the porcelain gadgets none became such a general

favourite in later times. The moulded form of the pipe-bowl is, of course, a long way behind the painted ornament. There is scarcely a subject which we do not find painted on the pipe-bowls of the Empire and *Biedermeier* periods, the latter especially: a "beautiful girl's head," nude women, hunting scenes, views, silhouettes, and badges. Finally to the pipe-bowl belongs the *Tabaksstopfer* which is mentioned in the Meissen price list in the form of *Jungfernbeinchen* ("maidens' legs"), *Lautpfeifgen* ("lutes"), and *Figürgen* ("little figures"). "Maidens' legs" of the rococo period are often charmingly modelled and painted with a pretty shoe. Later they were usually thicker, and the *Biedermeier* period rarely avoided the temptation to add a flea—a coarse joke.

FIG. 99. CANE-HEAD
Modelled by F. A. Bustelli. Nymphenburg; about 1760

Like the sword with a porcelain hilt, delicately modelled and beautifully painted, the walking-stick was part of the equipment of complete gentlemen in the eighteenth century, and consisted of a light cane of fine malacca with a knob or crook. These cane-knobs are often finely painted, and sometimes have rich moulding in relief as well (Figs. 98, 99). *Stockhaacken—i.e.*, crooks—were usually figurine in form. Nymphenburg produced charming little objects of this kind; the most beautiful are perhaps the Jew's head and the coquettish head of a girl with a rose in her hair, both modelled by the master hand of Bustelli (Fig. 98). Very fine *Stockhaacken* also came from the Berlin factory (Fig. 100). In which context we may remark that the practice of carrying walking-sticks was fashionable among ladies. Numerous portraits are known where ladies carry a stick in the hand as well as a sunshade.

If we leave out of account the *Camisol Knöpfgen*, or jacket buttons, which could be had at Meissen, but were naturally made in most other factories, this exhausts the series of porcelain 'gallantries' which were produced for the masculine world of the day. Far wider is the repertory of objects for the use of ladies. Of the decorative objects of the eighteenth century we need mention only *Ohr-Pendeloquen*, or ear-pendants (made at Meissen in sets of eight pieces), and *Ohr-Rosen* (ear-roses), and perhaps also *Kreuzlein zum Anhängen* (little crosses for pendants), which were made, for example, at Frankenthal. Special objects for needlework include thimbles, of which there are large numbers with miniature painting in a private collection at Frankfort, *Schützgen*, or shuttles, and *Seide-*

FIG. 100. CANE-HANDLE
Berlin; about 1770
Berlin, Schlossmuseum

windgen (silk-reels), known as *Garnwickler* at Frankenthal, needle-cases in the form of asparagus, figures, and babies, scissors-cases, with or without lid, and sponge-boxes, for a sponge soaked in perfume; the latter are mentioned at Nymphenburg in the form of an egg. The small *étuis* with snap-lid, to-day sometimes called *nécessaires*, were freely made everywhere; they kept together a number of little instruments such as ear-picks and scissors and a little ivory memorandum book. These objects may have been intended for use by both sexes; such, at any rate, were toothpick-cases, watch-stands, varying in price from 10 gulden at Nymphenburg to 20 thalers at Meissen, and, more especially, the little bottles described as *Spiritusfläschgen* in the Meissen price list. They were made with painting of flowers, fruit, landscapes, and figures in every conceivable style, and also in the form of figures, fruits, and animals. One of the favourite Meissen models, copied in nearly all European factories, is that of a monk carrying on his back a sheaf of corn, with a little girl concealed in it. Her head peeps out; it takes out and serves as a stopper. The English factory at Chelsea was very ingenious in devising such figurine bottles; hundreds of these tiny works of art were produced there (Figs. 102, 103) and often have short mottoes, mostly in French, alluding to the nature of the vessel, as *don d'amour* and *don d'amitié*.

If we mention *Couteau Griffe* ("knife-handles"), *Perlocken*

FIG. 101. MEISSEN FLASKS IN THE FORM OF MINIATURE FIGURES
Formerly in the Mühsam Collection, Berlin

("beads"), and the *Blümgen* ("flowers") attached to the bronze mounts of groups and to lustres, which were a speciality of Sèvres and Frankenthal, the 'gallantries' conclude the Meissen price list. It is doubtful whether the "Paternoster of sixty small beads and twelve large, with one cross," can be included in that category. Many other kinds of small objects were, of course, manufactured. Not only have they been preserved, but they are specifically mentioned in the records—*e.g.*, those of the Fürstenberg factory. They include the stands known as *Pompadour-Unterteile* with bulging sides and elaborate open-work decoration (though in many cases it is not quite certain whether they are not rather brush-backs), linen-slides and hat-buckles, crosses of orders, and bangles or bracelets, *Coulans*, or rings for purses, ring-stones with miniature portraits, chess sets and boxes of counters, also table-bells, of

FIG. 102. CHELSEA FLASKS
Hamburg, Otto Blohm Collection

which beautiful Meissen and Vienna specimens survive, *baignoirs*, or little eye-baths, and pomade- and rouge-pots. These last prepared the way for large toilet sets, complete with pots and boxes in great variety of forms, brushes, candlesticks, and mirrors. In Figs. 23 and 22 we illustrate two such sets of the early Meissen period; one has Imari decoration on a yellow ground, and is stated to have been made for the King, while the other has a soft grey-green ground with the double-eagle arms, and was made as a royal gift.

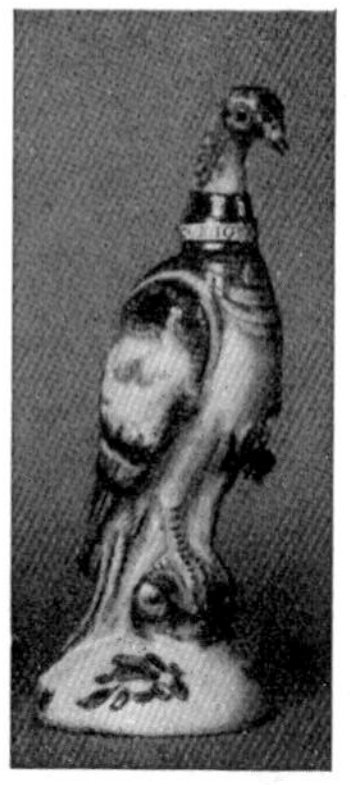

FIG. 103. CHELSEA FLASK IN THE FORM OF A BIRD
Hamburg, Otto Blohm Collection

Lastly we may mention here the use of porcelain for decorative panels in the form of rectangular tiles, as well as round, oval, and other flat shapes. These were intended for inlay in furniture, as in the Dubsky Room of Vienna porcelain already mentioned, and as in the many sumptuous examples of Sèvres manufacture. Small mural ornaments moulded with borders in relief and painted with portraits, landscapes, and mythological scenes were in favour in several factories, notably Fürstenberg and Volkstedt. Wall-brackets, with open-work and painted decoration, for the display of figures may be fittingly included among these decorative pieces.

CHAPTER IV

PORCELAIN FIGURES

I. Development of Technique and Style

When we discuss eighteenth-century porcelain to-day we involuntarily think first of figures rather than of vessels. The spirit of the age in all its phases, from loud-mouthed baroque to the coquetries of rococo, and from rococo again to the cool grace of Louis Seize, was never more truly expressed than in the multitude of porcelain figures issuing from the kilns of dozens of factories in thousands of different varieties. The high esteem which porcelain plastic enjoys to-day is indeed fully justified, for it is among porcelain figures that we find the highest achievement of plastic art in the eighteenth century. Nor is a critical estimate of this art in the least affected by the fact that porcelain figures were not made once and for all, but many times multiplied, so that they are in some sense an instance of mass-production. The glory of eighteenth-century sculpture does not lie in large-scale statuary, but in these small white glazed figures with colour-painting—*Puppen*, as they were called in Germany. They come from the hands of the most gifted plastic artists of the eighteenth century. A number of the most important porcelain-modellers had been originally sculptors; such were Kändler, Linck, and Beyer. Many of them regarded their work for the pottery and porcelain factories simply as a side-line, but with few exceptions posterity judges their powers not by their big statues, but by the eight-inch figures which they made for porcelain. The soul of eighteenth-century art is translated into porcelain. Rococo and porcelain are peers. A serious attempt has been made to show that rococo was derived from porcelain. But style and expression in porcelain plastic are a discovery of the baroque spirit. Strictly speaking, they are the creation of a brilliant sculptor who had a natural feeling for the monumental passion, the torrential pathos of baroque art. Johann Joachim Kändler is the real father of porcelain plastic. It is

FIG. 104. FIGURE FROM THE ITALIAN COMEDY IN BÖTTGER'S STONEWARE
Meissen; about 1715–20
Frankfort-on-the-Main, Kunstgewerbemuseum

true that even in the early period of the Meissen factory lively figures with a certain distinction of modelling were being made in the brown stoneware and in Böttger's early porcelain.

Such are the beautiful comedy figure in Fig. 104, the Chinaman in Fig. 105, and the Callot figure of Fig. 106. It is also true that several able modellers were working at Meissen before Kändler. But it was not until this young Court sculptor assumed control in the year 1731 that Meissen plastic started

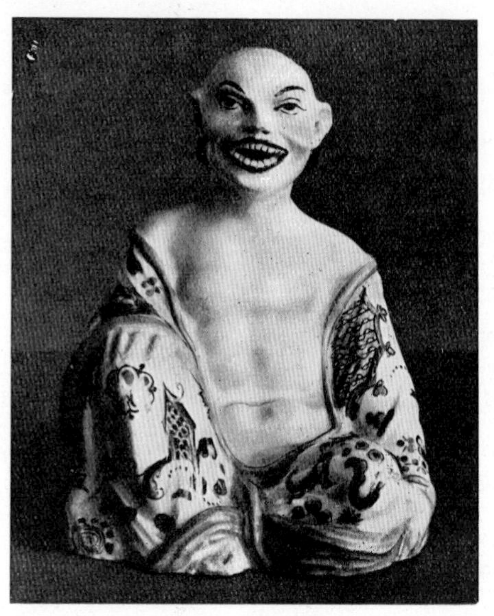

FIG. 105. CHINAMAN
Meissen; about 1720. See p. 243.
Mannheim, L. Hunig Collection

its amazing career; it swept on to a sovereignty which no other factory ever challenged.

There was the happiest combination of circumstances: on the one hand, a king who wanted his factory to make history, on the other, an artist whose execution was always outdoing the ambition of his master. When Kändler was engaged, work had already begun on the Japanese Palace. We have already referred to the grand scheme of Augustus the Strong for equipping the entire palace with a great series of vases, beasts, and figures. Before Kändler's appointment another and very capable artist, Gottlob Kirchner, had been working for several years on this great undertaking. We illustrate here one of his best works, the figure of St Paul the Apostle, made for the chapel of the Japanese Palace (Fig. 107). In the grand movement of its drapery and the quick turn of its expressive head this figure is a typical example of late baroque plastic. It is about three feet in height and, in common with other large pieces of this period, has the technical fault of numerous well-marked cracks. It was not safe to give these large figures a second firing, and con-

FIG. 106. CALLOT FIGURE
Meissen; about 1720. See p. 241.
Hamburg, Otto Blohm Collection

FIG. 107. PAUL THE APOSTLE
By G. Kirchner. Meissen; about 1732.
See p. 302.
Leipzig, Kunstgewerbemuseum

sequently they were all decorated with cold painting; but in most pieces this has disappeared. Other known works of Kirchner are large grotesque vases after designs by Jacques Stella (Paris, 1667), and also lively groups of animals. Two other works by him, which are important for the early history of Meissen plastic, are illustrated in Figs. 108 and 109: a big fountain with sumptuous painting in the style of Herold and a Nepomuk group on a high pedestal decorated

FIG. 108. FOUNTAIN
By G. Kirchner. Meissen; 1727–28. See p. 189.
Berlin, Schlossmuseum

FIG. 109. ST NEPOMUK
By G. Kirchner. Meissen; 1731. See pp. 189, 192.
Frankfort-on-the-Main, Kunstgewerbemuseum

with *Laub- und Bandelwerk*, executed in 1731—of course, from a foreign model. Kirchner, whose high qualities as

FIG. 110. PADUAN COCK
By J. J. Kändler. Meissen; about 1733
Dresden, Porzellansammlung

a modeller have been increasingly recognized of recent years, was now reinforced by young Kändler, with a view to speeding up the work for the Japanese Palace. It was soon evident that he was much the greater force. Kirchner felt he was out of the picture and resigned his job. Kändler now had a free hand, and henceforward was amazingly prolific. At this early period the main business of the factory was to provide large animal figures for the Japanese Palace. A considerable number of excellent groups and single beasts is preserved in the Johanneum, while occasional pieces passed at the sales of this collection to other museums and private collections. The Paduan cock illustrated in Fig. 110 gives an excellent idea of Kändler's art, its extraordinary vigour and its characteristic baroque stylization. In the following period Kändler modelled groups of many figures on a large scale; but his most ambitious, indeed astonishing, scheme was an equestrian statue of Augustus III in porcelain, to be made in separate parts and assembled with the aid of an iron framework. Some of the parts were actually made, but, although the technical difficulties were certainly overcome, the whole statue was never completed.

All this large statuary was, of course, produced not for reproduction and sale, but to flatter the prestige of the ruling house. At the same time work proceeded on the small figure models, which were intended for reproduction in large editions. There was, in fact, a technical reason for this transition from big statuary to figures of smaller size: the smaller the figure, the greater the prospect of a successful firing. It was this department of porcelain plastic that laid the foundations of Kändler's peculiar renown. Kändler here was the creator of an art, and all the work in groups and figures done by other factories is in the long run in Kändler's debt. He turned out model after model with an ease which is astonishing and an invention that never failed. The corpus of his work has never been collected, but in groups and figures alone a thousand works would scarcely be too high an estimate. In the whole ambit of representation in eighteenth-century porcelain there is scarcely a subject which was not treated by Kändler, scarcely even a subject for which he did not fix the paradigm. And when we remember, too, that Kändler was responsible for most of the vessel shapes of Meissen, particularly those of the famous services made for Count Brühl and Count Sulkowsky, we may indeed marvel at the prodigious fecundity of this extraordinary man.

Towards 1740, when Kändler was at the height of his powers,

FIG. 111. LADY WITH FAN
By J. J. Kändler. Meissen; about 1740. See p. 303.
Munich, Residenz

the baroque style, in which he had been brought up, entered its last phase of rococo. Kändler was himself one of the leaders of the movement, and he contributed not a little to the triumph of the new style. His figures are in a striking sense the crystallization of the new idea of life, its easy graces and its effortless superiority. In their beauty and their truth they are the perfect mirror of a life-loving and light-hearted age. High society, middle class, commonalty, appear before us in porcelain, and in flesh and blood, as they were never quite portrayed in the art of the painter or the engraver.

I do not intend to give here a close analysis of Kändler's

FIG. 112. PAIR OF LOVERS AT A SPINET
By J. J. Kändler. Meissen; about 1740
Munich, Residenz

style in figure-modelling. In contrast with the work of younger artists it never quite repudiated its origins in heavy, full-blooded baroque. The objects shown in Figs. 111–116 and in the Plate facing p. 162, all works by Kändler, serve to illustrate the amazing versatility and artistic power of this great master of little figures. But in the 1760's a change in style set in; Louis Seize was blowing up like a cool breeze from antiquity, and the ageing artist could not keep pace with a second change. Meissen was being overtaken by newer factories and younger artists, and, finding that both financially and artistic-

FIG. 113. CRINOLINE GROUP
By J. J. Kändler. Meissen; about 1740
Palace at Ansbach. Photo Stödtner

ally she was falling into the rear, she decided to call in a younger modeller from Paris, Michel Victor Acier, to bring fresh blood into the work of the factory. Kändler, however, retained till his death the supervision of the 'white gang.'

But the sovereignty of Meissen was gone past recall. In the period of fully developed rococo, roughly the decade 1755–65, other factories, especially several in the South of Germany,

FIG. 114. THE CURIOUS HARLEQUIN
By J. J. Kändler. Meissen; about 1740. See p. 262.
Formerly in the Mühsam Collection, Berlin

took the lead in the art of porcelain. In the front rank of them was Nymphenburg, a factory which may claim credit for the most notable plastic work in the mature rococo style. Here, again, we find a single outstanding artist, to whose career the

Bavarian factory owed its eminence. This man was Franz Anton Bustelli. In contrast with Kändler and many other modellers, very little is known of the details of his life. He is first mentioned at Neudeck in 1754, and apparently died at Nymphenburg in or shortly before 1763. His works are alive

FIG. 115. PAIR OF LOVERS
By J. J. Kändler. Meissen; about 1745. See p. 268.
Hamburg, Museum für Kunst und Gewerbe

with Southern temperament, but it is uncertain whether his training as an artist was received in Italy. His work shows such similarities with Bavarian wood-sculpture of the rococo period that we may regard him with some confidence as a German artist. We can, in fact, watch the development of his style as he passes from the clumsy modelling of his early work, to reach a brilliant maturity in the medium of porcelain.

As an artist Bustelli is the antithesis of Kändler. Kändler, with his love for strong form and an ample sweep of drapery, presents real live people; Bustelli makes his figures slim and supple, defining the draw of his drapery by sharp folds and wrinkles, and reducing his formal appeal to a moment of vivid

FIG. 116. FREEMASON
By J. J. Kändler. Meissen; about 1740
Dresden, Porzellansammlung

expression. Kändler's creatures enjoy rude health and a good circulation. Bustelli's are ladies and gentlemen, always sensitive and over-educated, with an elegance that is all gesture and excitement, and poses that never fail to express. In every inclination of a head, in the nice poise of a hand, in every bending of a limb is the wild genius of Bustelli, always breaking in, always bursting with surprises. The groups and figures here illustrated need no commentary. His mastery of large-scale portraiture is shown by the astoundingly powerful bust of Count Sigismund von Haimhausen (Fig. 139), who was the real founder of the Nymphenburg factory.

We may call attention at this point to a superficial, but not

FIG. 117. MINERS
Miessen; about 1745. See p. 253.
Mannheim, Hermannsdorf Collection

unimportant, difference of style between the early models and the majority of the rococo figures which we have been discussing. In the early Kändler models the pedestal is simply an irregular base, round or oval in shape, and carpeted with gay flowers and green leaves in relief. Towards the middle of the eighteenth century Kändler himself introduced a new type of design, which became law and ordinance to porcelain-modellers for the best part of a generation. *Rocaille* work, the typical decorative form of rococo, was introduced on the pedestal, and it was not long before the entire base was composed of similar scroll forms played into a lively rhythm. Bustelli preferred flat pedestals with scrolls lightly trimmed in colour to give life and movement, and he went so far as to

FIG. 118. LADY SPINNING
Meissen; about 1750. See pp. 303–304.
Formerly in the Mühsam Collection, Berlin

make the *rocaille* work an intrinsic element in the design of the group, as may be seen in Figs. 136 and 137. This method had many attractions, and created a following in most other factories of South Germany: we find it also at Frankenthal and Ludwigsburg, but never such spirited treatment as Bustelli's.

Of the tendency in base form during the next period we shall have something to say in due course.

Other modellers who worked at Nymphenburg after the death of Bustelli—*e.g.*, Dominikus Auliczek—produced nothing

FIG. 119. CHINESE LADY AND CHILDREN
Meissen; middle of the eighteenth century. See p. 310.
Formerly in the Mühsam Collection, Berlin

to compare with the masterpieces of this happy modeller; just as at Meissen Kändler was a long way ahead of all his colleagues. At Frankenthal the talents were more equally distributed among the various modellers, even though the art of Konrad Linck was by a long way its most notable achievement. Frankenthal plastic begins in a heavy, powerful style with the works of Johann Wilhelm Lanz. The *Mort Group* shown in Fig. 140 had been modelled by him during his Strasburg period—that is, before 1755. It is found with the plain base typical of Strasburg. But in the example illustrated

FIG. 120. GROUP OF CHINAMAN AND CHILDREN
Meissen; middle of the eighteenth century
Formerly in the Mühsam Collection, Berlin

it has the *rocaille* base, which was the rule at Frankenthal from the outset until the 1770's. The charming little minuet dancer in Fig. 141 is also by Lanz. Next come the figures of Johann Friedrich Lück, a modeller who had previously worked at Meissen. They are a trifle stiff, but fresh in invention (Figs. 142 and 143). The year 1762 saw the appointment of Konrad

Linck. He had attended the Vienna Academy and had worked at Berlin and Potsdam. Henceforward he defined and perfected the style of Frankenthal, and at Frankenthal he was the man responsible for the decisive change from rococo to classicism. His sense of form is quite different from Bustelli's, but he has nevertheless a certain affinity with him, and he is

FIG. 121. TOILET SCENE
Meissen; about 1750
Palace at Ansbach

by far the most brilliant representative of the period of transition. The decorative grace of his beautiful small heads has scarcely been surpassed, and his groups are a fine orchestration of lusty nudities. Figs. 144–146 illustrate his distinctive style. The large allegorical group in Fig. 147 is not very happily conceived, but its subject, of which something will be said later, cramped his style hopelessly; and we must remember that the group did not appear until 1775.

A much more prolific artist than Linck was Karl Gottlieb

FIG. 122. FIGURES OF ARTISANS
By J. J. Kändler. Meissen; about 1750
Formerly in the Mühsam Collection, Berlin

Lück. He was apparently a cousin of Johann Friedrich Lück, and was working at Frankenthal before Linck's time. When

FIG. 123. CAVALIER
By J. J. Kändler. Meissen; 1754. See p. 251.
Formerly in the Mühsam Collection, Berlin

the latter migrated to Mannheim in 1766 he succeeded to his position as head modeller. He was an artist of extraordinary versatility, but was strongly influenced by the more important Linck, so that it is often difficult to distinguish the work of the

FIG. 124. LADY
By J. J. Kändler. Meissen; 1754. See p. 251.
Formerly in the Mühsam Collection, Berlin

two modellers. Lück's varied talents give his works a special interest as a mirror of contemporary society (see Figs. 149–153).

The later period of Frankenthal is represented by the models of J. P. Melchior; he came from Höchst, and I shall give a more detailed account of him under the head of that factory.

FIG. 125. QUACK DOCTOR
Meissen; middle of the eighteenth century
Formerly in the Mühsam Collection, Berlin

There were several excellent artists at work at Ludwigsburg, but no one has yet succeeded in distinguishing their works with any certainty. This factory attained its zenith during its early period. After a short devotion to pure rococo the *haute époque* of the factory began about 1760, but lasted less than ten years. This was the period of its best modellers,

FIG. 126. SHEPHERDESS
By J. J. Kändler. Meissen; 1750–60
Hamburg, Museum für Kunst und Gewerbe

Domenico Ferretti and, more especially, Wilhelm Beyer, both of whom were influenced by the first hints of a classical revival. In neither of them do we find the twittering excitement and easy pliancy of Bustelli models—only an academic chill. Beyer's *Lady taking Coffee* (Fig. 160) has some power of rhythm, but the artificial contrasts in the movements of the

FIG. 127. SHEPHERD
By J. J. Kändler. Meissen; 1750–60
Hamburg, Museum für Kunst und Gewerbe

limbs, body, and head are part of a formula which is repeated in hundreds of other groups and figures. We are a long way from the playful naturalness and conscious grace of Bustelli. Another marked change is extrinsic to the actual figure. The

The Startled Sleeper
By F. A. Bustelli. Nymphenburg; about 1760
Munich, Bayerisches National-Museum

rocaille base, which had been in vogue at Ludwigsburg from the earliest years of the factory, is now replaced by a rock-work pedestal decorated in colours, or a white rectangular plinth which gradually became the standard base form. It made porcelain figures look more like statues.

I cannot discuss here the peculiarities of every factory and every modeller. The purpose of this book is not to educate experts, but simply to stimulate interest, and to give in broad outline the essential facts in the history of porcelain. The other factories founded during the reign of rococo, Vienna, Berlin, Höchst, Fürstenberg, besides Ansbach, Kelsterbach, Fulda, and the rest, all began with a rococo style, and varied it delightfully according to the temperaments and skill of their artist modellers. All of them went over to the classical style. Some of them were quick on the new fashion; others hated it and took their time. Thus we often find surprising inconsistencies, and at times it is very difficult to fix the equation of date and style.

FIG. 128. MINIATURE FIGURES
Meissen; about 1750
Formerly in the Mühsam Collection, Berlin

Most of the big factories reached their zenith in the 1760's, but a few factories had to wait until about 1770 for the modellers who made at once their factory's style and their own reputations. Of these Höchst is the chief name. In Feilner and, especially, in Russinger this factory already possessed two notable modellers whose sense of form was both excellent and original (Fig. 164); but it got its definitive style from Johann Peter Melchior (Figs. 165–170). Melchior's attitude towards art was throughout influenced by France, as also was Beyer's, and he made a refinement of classicism or Louis Seize. This classical revival—that is to say, this reaction against the extravagance of rococo—was of diverse origins, not the least important being the influence of literature and philosophy. The great scholar and champion of antiquity J. J. Winckelmann was one of the first to assail rococo—"the scrolls and inevitable shell-work which ornament can never escape"—and he broke his stick on our present subject. "Porcelain," said he, "is nearly always made into idiotic puppets." In matters of art he was *præceptor Germaniæ*. From the west of Europe he echoed Rousseau's battle-cry against the tyranny of courts, his defence of the middle classes, and the 'return to nature.' Gessner had written his *Idylls*, and then came Goethe with his *Leiden des jungen Werther*. In England Wordsworth delivered himself of the same message, and the noble savage became a Lakeland peasant. At the same time Winckelmann's 'beauty' had become a gospel as well as an æsthetic, and men like Robert Adam, Sir William Hamilton, Flaxman, and Wedgwood were full of an 'admiration' for antique severity, not different in quality from the romantic awe for the sublimity of waterfalls. All of which ended the naughty adventures of "the smiling shepherdesses," and put in their place "a purer Artemis, a virgin Cleopatra, a nobler nymph-hood," as they were made famous in the work of Beyer at Ludwigsburg.

FIG. 129. PERFUME-BURNER
Meissen; about 1750
Berlin, Schlossmuseum

Melchior was in direct contact with the young Goethe. There exists a fine portrait of the poet by Melchior, with the following dedication: "The poet of the *Sorrows of Young*

Werther by his friend Melchior, done from the life." It is thus scarcely surprising that Melchior absorbed the spirit of the new movement.

FIG. 130. ANNETTE AND LUBIN
Meissen; about 1780. See pp. 270–271.
Hamburg, Museum für Kunst und Gewerbe

From 1766 to 1779 he was working for the Höchst factory, and there are numerous models to illustrate his industry and his tireless ingenuity. In spite of all differences of subject there is scarcely an artist in porcelain whose works present so strong a family likeness. He lacked the sweeping precision of a Kändler. He has not the wayward energy of Bustelli. In grace and elegance he will not compare with Konrad Linck.

FIG. 131. PAIR OF MINUET DANCERS
By F. A. Bustelli. Nymphenburg; about 1755. See p. 260 *et seq.*
Munich, Bayerisches National-Museum

He is just a pleasant, jolly middle-class creature with a weakness for sentimentality, and he appears as such in his choice of subjects. The brilliant courts of Augustus the Strong and Charles Eugene of Württemberg no longer threw their shadows over Höchst. The Italian comedy, which had captured Munich in Bustelli's time, had ended its mad revels, and in its place people listened to French operas full of pretty sentiments, and waxed enthusiastic over Daphnis and Chloe.

FIG. 132. FIGURE FROM THE ITALIAN COMEDY
Modelled by F. A. Bustelli. Nymphenburg; about 1760.
See p. 262.
Frankfort-on-the-Main, Kunsgewerbemuseum

Kändler had portrayed artisans, peasants, beggars, simply as members of the great society; the classical revival sentimentalized them. The figures of such people reek of didacticism and sentimental uplift. The subject dearest to Melchior's heart, and one he was never tired of exploring, was the world of childhood, sometimes a naïve world, at times rather a stagy world. Where once had been fat impossible cherubs, or *putti*, there are now "golden lads and girls." Where there had once been pretty allegories we find peasant

FIG. 133. FIGURES FROM THE ITALIAN COMEDY
By F. A. Bustelli. Nymphenburg; about 1760. See p. 262.
Munich, Bayerisches National-Museum

children of flesh and blood. Besides all this, Melchior's work is full of the popular classical mythology which throughout the eighteenth century had been almost inbred. He had also a strong liking for exotic subjects, and designed them with the freedom of a master; his delightful Turks and his Chinese scenes are among his most vigorous works. The bases of Melchior's figures are also characteristic, and not to be confused with the work of any other factory. It goes without saying that at this date there is no more *rocaille* work. His bases are made of superimposed layers of rock covered with a wide expanse of grass overhanging the sides. Here again we

FIG. 134. CHINAMAN
By F. A. Bustelli. Nymphenburg; about 1760
Munich, Bayerisches National-Museum

find the 'return to nature' in a detail external to the figure itself. Equally characteristic is the treatment of colour in Höchst figures, but I shall refer to this in a later connexion.

Following precedent, I have dealt only with Melchior, but he is more or less typical. Recent researches seem to prove a number of different hands in works which have hitherto been ascribed to Melchior alone. In any case it is clear that the share of Laurentius Russinger must not be underestimated.

Indeed, he seems to have fixed the type of 'Melchior' figures before Melchior himself came to Höchst. There are many other difficulties in the way of scientific study of the early period of Höchst, though it is full of interest and variety. This is not the place to discuss such problems; but the illustrations

FIG. 135. CHINESE WOMAN
By F. A. Bustelli. Nymphenburg; about 1760
Munich, Bayerisches National-Museum

(Figs. 165–170) will give some idea at least of Höchst productions after Melchior joined the factory. *The Old Coquette* (Fig. 171), according to the evidence of an engraving by Göz dated 1783, must have been produced immediately after Melchior left the factory. Nevertheless it well illustrates the refined and almost impersonal tradition of Höchst figures.

About the time that Melchior was working in the West of Germany a very similar style of porcelain was in vogue on the Danube—that is to say, at Vienna. Here the general tendency to classicism is marked by a type of sentiment peculiar to Vienna. The early period of the Vienna factory had produced little original work in the way of figures, but during the 1760's and 1770's there appeared a charming series of groups and figures, probably by the modeller Leopold Dannhauser,

FIG. 136. THE JEALOUS GALLANT
By F. A. Bustelli. Nymphenburg; about 1760
Munich, Bayerisches National-Museum

and happily uniting a certain coquettish grace with a Viennese sense of comfort and comeliness (Figs. 172–176). The Vienna master who best represents the developed classical style is Anton Grassi. He was a pupil of Beyer of Ludwigsburg, who since 1769 had been settled at Vienna as a sculptor, but he was chiefly influenced by the French school. He produced beautiful little works of art, such as the portrait scene in Fig. 177, which may rank with the finest work dating from the end of the eighteenth century.

As I have said, I have no intention of discussing in detail the figure plastic of all the German factories, but I may refer any who are interested to numerous special monographs which cover most of them. The illustrations to this book only give certain types of the various factories, and a few examples of them, and in accordance with the scheme of the book they have been selected on their own merits as works of art. It has only been possible to allot a few illustrations to other than German factories (Figs. 197–201). In this, the English, edition these have been supplemented by a few English figures. They have been selected likewise on their own merits, but also to give some idea of English plastic in contrast with that of Germany (Figs. 40, 43, 44, 46, 47, 54–57, 59, 62).

I need only add in conclusion that towards the end of the eighteenth century white unpainted porcelain, especially unglazed biscuit, became more and more fashionable. One cause of this vogue was the influence of ancient marbles; another was the example of the Sèvres factory, which had used biscuit for all its figure work since about 1750 (Figs. 200, 201). A characteristic example of the frigid manner appears in Fig. 163, a family monument made at Ludwigsburg for the director of the factory, von Kaufmann, and his two wives and seven children. The pretty *genre* group in Fig. 184 dates from the year 1800, and is the work of Riese, the head modeller at Berlin. Thereby hangs a pleasant tale of the Hohenzollerns. Frederick the Great took a ball from the Prince Frederick William, afterwards Frederick William II. The boy begged impetuously to have his ball again; whereupon the old King remarked: "You shan't have your Silesia back again!"

2. The Painting of Figures

It may be taken as a general rule that all eighteenth-century porcelain was intended for painting. An exception must, of course, be made of the unglazed biscuit figures whose effect depended on their statuesque whiteness, but, as I have pointed out already, they did not appear in Germany until the last thirty years of the eighteenth century. They

FIG. 137. TURKISH LADY AND GENTLEMAN AT COFFEE
By F. A. Bustelli. Nymphenburg; about 1760
Cf. Figs. 134, 135, where the same models appear as Chinese.
Munich, Residenz

came in under the influence of Sèvres, and during the Empire period were made in larger numbers. We may assume, and the evidence of actual pieces tends to confirm the assumption, that most of the white glazed figures are in the nature of imperfect pieces which went wrong or cracked during the

FIG. 138. THE STORMY WOOING
Nymphenburg; about 1760
Munich, Bayerisches National-Museum

firing. They were regarded as wasters, and were sold off cheap. The number of unpainted pieces which have come down to us has sadly diminished in recent years, but this is to be explained by the fact that many white figures have lately acquired a cloak of many colours in the kilns of clever fakers.

The equal partnership of painting and modelling in the perfect unity of a work of art was a response to the taste of the

FIG. 139. PORTRAIT HEAD OF COUNT HAIMHAUSEN
By F. A. Bustelli. Nymphenburg; about 1760
Munich, Bayerisches National-Museum

eighteenth century. For later generations the painting is of the utmost importance, since more truthfully than all other works of fine and applied art it gives an idea of the colour taste of the age and the coloured effect of its costume.

FIG. 140. MORT GROUP
By J. W. Lanz. Frankenthal; about 1760. See p. 275.
Formerly in the Mühsam Collection, Berlin

The fact has only lately been emphasized that the modellers had considerable influence on the painting or embellishment (*Staffierung*) of their figures. At least, the more important modellers did. And it would, in fact, be quite unnatural to suppose that the modeller was content to give his figure only its naked shape, and that its future and fulfilment were matters of indifference to him. An architect might as well finish the brick-work of his house and leave the style of mouldings or paint-work to the discretion of his decorator. The eighteenth century, of all periods, had too much respect for the essential

FIG. 141. THE LITTLE DANCER
By J. W. Lanz. Frankenthal; about 1760
Formerly in the Mühsam Collection, Berlin

unity of a work of art. We may therefore take it as certain that Kändler, Bustelli, Melchior, were in direct, and directing, contact with the painting rooms of their respective factories, and that the embellishers took their counsel and followed their advice for the proper colouring of a particular figure. Otherwise it is impossible to account for the distinctive colouring in, say, Kändler figures. Both in general treatment and in details they are quite unlike the style of painting introduced by Herold.

FIG. 142. CAVALIER AND LADY WITH MUFFS
By J. F. Lück. Frankenthal; about 1760
Mannheim, C. Baer Collection

As the style of figure-modelling changed in the course of ten years the treatment of the colour changed with it. Meissen figures and groups of the first great Kändler period, eloquent in every gesture and every movement of the power and passion of baroque, show a palette of amazing brilliance that rejoices in the riot of colour (see Plate facing p. 162). A rich blue, a sap green, a smooth warm yellow, and a deep lustrous black fight for the ascendant, but readily combine in an orchestration of colour that is at once effective and restrained. The tempestuous crinolines of the ladies and the sleek suitings and mantles of the gentlemen are covered with broad sweeps of unbroken colour, and in the most beautiful pieces the heavy silks of the ladies' dresses are adorned with large flowered designs,

FIG. 143. THE DANCING LESSON
By J. F. Lück. Frankenthal; about 1760
Mannheim, C. Baer Collection

often on a rich black ground, and in striking contrast with the brilliant white or pale yellow of the underskirt.

The treatment of the base is also characteristic. The broad green leaves and brightly coloured flowers are flecked with patches of cold white ground, and so serve as a prelude and a foil to the ample surfaces and strong colours of the figure itself. Kändler and the transition to rococo changed all this in a moment. We find a like transformation in the other factories as well as at Meissen. It exploded the grand manner and organ utterance of baroque. In the rococo age you made polite conversation in a cultured tone, and did your under-

FIG. 144. BOREAS AND OREITHYIA
By K. Linck. Frankenthal; about 1770
Mannheim, C. Baer Collection

lining, not by thumping the table, but with your eyes. The first Frederick enjoyed beer and tobacco with his generals. Frederick the Great played the flute to his intimate friends.

FIG. 145. MELEAGER AND ATALANTA
By K. Linck. Frankenthal; about 1770
Munich, Residenz

The revolution in taste was, in fact, world-wide, and may be observed in every phase of contemporary life; and naturally it affected the sense of colour. People felt that the strong colours hitherto in vogue were too loud, and judicious between-shades took their place. A symptom of the change is the disappear-

FIG. 146. CLOCK WITH FIGURES
By K. Linck. Frankenthal; about 1770
Berlin, Mühsam Collection

ance of black. It was now used only where it was necessary: for shoes, hats, and buckles, in little specks, like patches on a lady's face. In other cases, such as some of the figures from the *commedia dell' arte*, it was part of a tradition and could not be avoided. The revolution in colour is already evident in the work of Bustelli (Plate facing p. 210), almost all the primary colours being used in delicate shades. Iron red, which was used by Kändler to give the rich bloom of the pomegranate, is quieter and more delicate. Purple is paler, and yellow has a colder tone. The general scheme of colours was enlivened by exposing as much as possible of the unpainted surface, so as to give full effect to the white sheen of the glaze. From the 1750's onwards the same principle was followed in all other factories. The Frankenthal group of goatherd and

FIG. 147. VOTA PALATINATUS EXAUDITA
By K. Linck. Frankenthal; about 1775. See pp. 283–284.
Frankfort-on-the-Main, Kunstgewerbemuseum

shepherdess in the Plate facing p. 252 is further proof of this. The black is confined to the feet, eyes, and horns of the kid lying in front of them—in this case there was no other need for it. Elsewhere we find only shade colours, pale purple and tints of blue, green, and yellow. The costumes are flowered, partly to avoid expanses of monochrome surface, and partly to render in paint the mood of glitter and gaiety which has given to the *rocaille* background the naughty flourish of a foaming wave. Light flowered silks were the fashionable material of the age. The walls of the *salon*, stripped of the heavy colour of baroque, were livelier to live in and gay with mirrors. Its furniture was moulded in interesting curves, and fashionable artists painted portraits of its brilliant throng in the soft and fragrant colours of pastel.

The succeeding age and the style of Louis Seize are less important for the colouring of porcelain. Quiet between-shades still predominate, but here and there we find a touch of stronger colour. In particular, the available surface was filled in more freely, and the white ground of the glaze was not used with the same assertion. Of this tendency Melchior is a good example. The difference of style may perhaps be pointed by saying that the rococo painter painted porcelain, whereas Melchior stroked it. There are no more specks of white on the grassy base. The costumes are conceived as coloured materials, usually self-coloured and often flowered, but as a rule the airy broadcast flowers are replaced by solemn striped patterns, which had lately come into fashion. Indeed, the new taste in colour and the new naturalism went to such lengths that the exposed parts of the figure, face, hands, feet, and even the whole body, were covered with a rosy flesh tint; whereas the previous generation had confined itself to little touches of rouge on the cheeks, lips, nostrils, and in the corners of the eyes, which served to set off the brilliant white of the face. As a rule Melchior used only shade colours. His figures can be recognized yards away by the predominance of a light, rather sickly, rose pink. As the eighteenth century draws to its close the painting at Höchst, Frankenthal, Ludwigsburg, Berlin, and elsewhere again becomes more

FIG. 148. MOUSE
Frankenthal; about 1770
Formerly in the Mühsam Collection, Berlin

FIG. 149. SET OF HUNTING FIGURES KNOWN AS "JÄGER AUS KURPFALZ"
By K. G. Lück. Frankenthal; about 1765. See p. 275.
Mannheim, C. Baer Collection

powerful, and the palette darker and dirtier. We often find patterns of black dots and rigid stripes or squares, which would have been æsthetically impossible twenty-five years earlier.

Thus the painting of figures was perfectly in accord with

FIG. 150. CONCORD IN MARRIAGE
By K. G. Lück. Frankenthal; about 1765. See p. 253.
Mannheim, C. Baer Collection

the change in plastic style which has been described above. Within the limits of period painting each factory naturally had its own idioms of colour and motive. They are often so obvious that with a little practice it is quite easy to assign a figure or group to the factory of its origin. The broadcast flowers on Meissen drapery are quite different from those of Frankenthal. The tiny purple blooms of early Höchst are also found on Frankenthal, but they were certainly introduced by an artist who migrated from Höchst to the Palatinate. Quite different again is the note of colour in the flower-painting of Kloster-Veilsdorf. Similar idioms may be noted in

FIG. 151. DISCORD IN MARRIAGE
By K. G. Lück. Frankenthal; about 1765. See p. 253.
Mannheim, C. Baer Collection

the treatment of the hair and eyes: thus, round black pupils are characteristic of Höchst figures of the 1770's and 1780's, while Ansbach productions, with a few exceptions, can be detected by the redness of the eyes.

A further fact which has an important bearing on the artistic value of a piece, and consequently on its price in the market of to-day, can be established by the style of the painting. I mean the date. Many groups and figures were reproduced again and again, and at long intervals of time;

FIG. 152. GROUP REPRESENTING ARCHITECTURE
By K. G. Lück. Frankenthal; about 1770
Formerly in the Mühsam Collection, Berlin

but here the style of the painting provides a definite criterion of whether the figure in question is early or late.

3. Range of Subjects

The cultural history of porcelain has yet to be written. Such an inquiry would answer a question of some importance —the exact place of porcelain in the art of the eighteenth

FIG. 153. A CHINESE HOUSE
By K. G. Lück. Frankenthal; about 1770
Munich, Residenz

century. It would also throw surprising lights on the art and society, spirit and history, of an age which is full of difficulties. The eighteenth century was born in the blaze of divine monarchy. It died in the promise and performance of de-

FIG. 154. GROUP OF BALLET-DANCERS
Ludwigsburg; about 1760. See pp. 269–270.
Mannheim, C. Baer Collection

mocracy. It passed from the divinity of kings to the sanctity of parliaments. It saw the birth of Gottsched and the childhood of Heine. It contains Mozart and Beethoven as well as Bach and Händel. It stretches from Dryden to Coleridge, from St Paul's to the Adelphi. There is no end to its contrasts.

It has its great names: Augustus the Strong, Frederick the

Great, Marie-Antoinette; its great mistresses: Aurora von Königsmarck, Mme Pompadour, Franziska von Hohenheim; its alchemists and adventurers: Böttger, Casanova, Cagliostro. With its quaint echoes of a festive world this wonderful century

FIG. 155. PAIR OF DANCERS IN PEASANT COSTUME TAKING OFF THEIR MASKS
Ludwigsburg; about 1765. See p. 256.
Formerly in the Mühsam Collection, Berlin

is presented to us in porcelain. The film may be a coloured one, but it is true to life.

Porcelain figures were articles of luxury, and in the nature of the case they show us only the sunshine; war and misery, poverty and sickness, were outside their programme. The repertory of the modeller embraced every sphere of life from the palace to the cottage. It included not only the pleasures of society, such as music and dancing, the theatre and the chase, but mythology, allegory, 'sensation,' and anything else that interested the world which he portrayed. In the sequel

FIG. 156. CHINESE PRINCE
Probably by D. Ferretti. Ludwigsburg; about 1763
Stuttgart, Schlossmuseum

I can describe only a few types of subject, which were of special interest to the art of porcelain, and I do not claim either fullness or order.

(A) *Dwarfs and Fools*

Peculiar figures of dwarfs, one of which is illustrated in Fig. 106, appear at the very beginning of modelling in porcelain, with the early period of Meissen. The eighteenth century had a bent for satire, and a wholesome, not to say disgusting, appetite for the ludicrous and the grotesque; so that hunchbacks and dwarfs appealed to it very strongly. A book published at Amsterdam in 1716, entitled *Il Calotto resuscitato. Oder Neu eingerichtes Zwerchen Cabinet*, with the bilingual subtitle *Le monde est plein de sots joieux. Les plus Petits sont les mieux; De Waereld ist vol Gekken-Nesten de Klynste Narren zyn de beste*,[1] must have enjoyed a wide popularity. Callot figures were modelled not only at Meissen, but at Vienna and Venice, and in the second half of the eighteenth century travelled even farther—*e.g.*, to Höchst. There exists a considerable number of these figures modelled after *Il Calotto resuscitato.* In all of them the type of the figure is explained in grotesque inscriptions or comic verses. Fig. 106 shows Don Miguel de Zorrero; and in a later edition, published at Augsburg, he is given the following description:

Don Miguel Zorrero Fuerto Cauallero de las Trençadas de çapatos, Padre del gran Cap°. Couiello, Pariente de Don Quixote, Gouernador en las Tierras Australes desconocidas.

Es ist zwar nie erhört, niemand hats dahin bracht,
Das Er in einem Land sich Souverain gemacht.
So weder Er, noch sonst ein Mensch auf Erd gesehen,
Allein Ich, der die Welt nach Wunsch mit List kan drehen,
Hab durch Verstand und Starck, Bravour und rahren Witz,
In der Australen Land gebracht den Herren-Sitz.

In the English this runs as follows:

Don Miguel Zorrero, a fiery gentleman with braided shoes, father of the great Captain Coviello, kinsman of Don Quixote, ruler of the unknown Southern Lands.

A thing beyond contrivance, a quite unheard of thing,
For any man, in any land, to make himself a king.
Not this, nor that, nor any man in all the world, but I,
Who give my bias to the world, alone, by being sly,
By science, strength, and valour, by my superhuman brain,
Have won myself in Southern Land a nobleman's domain.

[1] *The Callot Reviv'd, or a New Cabinet of Dwarfs.*
Merry fools on earth abound,
The smallest will the best be found.

The two Court dwarfs of Augustus the Strong, Joseph Fröhlich and the merry postmaster Schmiedel, acquired equal fame, and were perpetuated by the art of Kändler. He modelled them separately as busts and figures, and together in a group, and in the form of a pipe-bowl. We shall

FIG. 157. CHINESE GENTLEMAN IN AN ARBOUR
Ludwigsburg; about 1760–65
Stuttgart, Schlossmuseum

not be far wrong in suspecting that this was by direct command of the King. At a later date these Court dwarfs went out of fashion.

(B) *Chinamen and Turks*

The Chinamen who superseded the dwarfs and fools had an important place in the repertory of all factories. I have already referred to the important influence of the Far East on

European art and civilization during the greater part of the eighteenth century. The earliest Meissen figures were copied from Chinese porcelain figures, especially the small nodding 'pagodas' with perforated mouth and ears, used as incense-burners (Fig. 105). They appear next as pure figures, but

FIG. 158. CHINESE LADY IN AN ARBOUR
Ludwigsburg; about 1760–65
Stuttgart, Schlossmuseum

seen through European spectacles and remodelled in the grotesque shapes of *chinoiserie*, as they can be seen again in the painting of Herold. In the great early period of Meissen Kändler produced magnificent Chinese figures. Two fine groups, dating from the middle of the eighteenth century, are illustrated in Figs. 119 and 120. We also find them at Frankenthal and Ludwigsburg (Figs. 153, 156–158), and again at Nymphenburg, where Bustelli showed his usual grace and finish in the modelling of 'Chinamen' (Figs. 134.

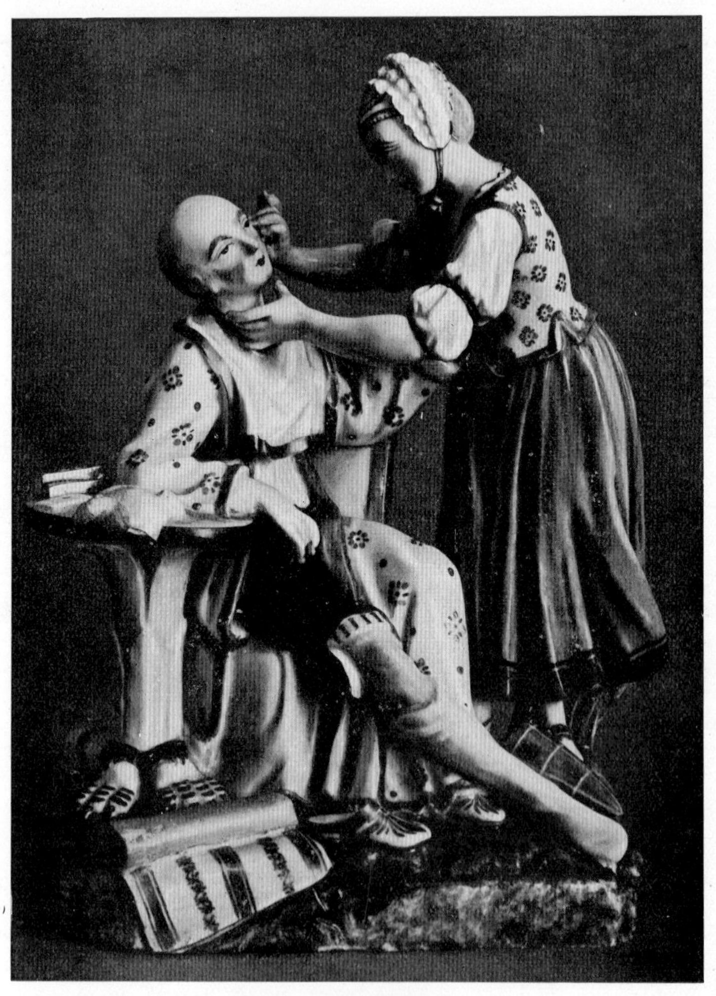

FIG. 159. THE SHAVE
Ludwigsburg; about 1765. See p. 253.
Mannheim, C. Baer Collection

135). It is extraordinary that at a time when painted *chinoiseries* and 'Indian' flower-painting were rapidly going out of fashion figure-modelling still preferred Far Eastern subjects until the time of Elias Meyer at Berlin (Fig. 183) and

FIG. 160. LADY TAKING COFFEE
By W. Beyer. Ludwigsburg; about 1765
Hamburg, Museum für Kunst und Gewerbe

Melchior at Höchst. The latter's great *Chinese Emperor* is the last and perhaps the most beautiful metamorphosis of China.

Of other exotic peoples the Turks may be specially mentioned. They are often found in porcelain. The beautiful Bustelli group in Fig. 137 appears in the Nymphenburg price list of 1767 as *Türk und Türkin beym Caffee Tisch* ("Turkish

FIG. 161. BOOTH AT A FAIR: "MARCHAND DE MODE"
Ludwigsburg; about 1765. See pp. 254–256.
Hamburg, Otto Blohm Collection

Lady and Gentleman at Coffee,") and shows the interest in the Turkish national drink, which at that time had become fashionable in Europe. The Copenhagen group with the eunuch (Fig. 198) is conceived with ethnographical precision, but in many other Turkish figures (from Meissen, Höchst, and other factories) it is highly probable that the subject is not a

FIG. 162. BOOTHS AND FIGURES AT A FAIR
By J. J. Louis. Ludwigsburg; about 1765
Stuttgart, Schlossmuseum

real Turk, but a European dressed up for a masquerade. This is also the case with many representations of other foreign peoples, so far as they are not definite national types in a stereotyped political *ensemble*, like the specimens of Russian peasantry in the Berlin table-centre made for Catherine the Great of Russia.

(C) *Nobles, Merchants, Peasants*

Innumerable figures are taken from the life and activities of contemporary society. Here again the fashion was started and set by Meissen—that is to say, by Kändler. He was constantly working for the King and the Court, and once he began to do *genre* scenes from the life of the times it was natural that he should find his themes in the society of the Court. It was equally natural, in an age which had no inhibitions and knew how to enjoy itself, that sex-appeal was of paramount importance. It is thus very creditable to Kändler that his numerous loving couples never became coarse or lewd—these are qualities we find in the smug propriety of the *Biedermeier* period. On the contrary, his charming romantic pieces are executed with the piquant humour and the exquisite irony of the fashionable world. It was Kändler who laid his finger on such themes, who saw, for example, a fine plastic opportunity in the swaying immobility of the huge crinolines which were then fashionable. That alone is enough to put him in the front rank of eighteenth-century sculptors. The whole of Court society, ladies and fine gentlemen, pages, Moors, ladies' maids, served him as models for innumerable groups and figures. In this connexion it is worth noting that few of the figures are pure inventions; they refer nearly always to some fact of contemporary life. The figures are always conceived as 'pendants,' though the allusion is only vaguely suggested.

Some authorities have wished to look for actual portraits among the numerous groups and figures. Many of them certainly are based on actual events, on those interesting occurrences which Court gossip enjoys and passes on. In certain cavalier figures we may think we recognize the features of

FIG. 163. FAMILY MONUMENT
Ludwigsburg; 1789. See p. 220.
Frankfort-on-the-Main, Kunstgewerbemuseum

Augustus the Strong himself. But the great majority of the figures cannot be regarded in any sense as portraits. Pretty

FIG. 164. GROUP KNOWN AS "THE LITTLE SULTAN"
Höchst; about 1760
Frankfort-on-the-Main, Historisches Museum

legends have gathered round various Kändler groups. Thus, the beautiful group in Fig. 113 'must' represent the "Mad Margrave," Karl Wilhelm of Ansbach, presenting his mistress with a gingerbread heart which he had purchased from a peddling woman, not knowing that she was his wife in disguise. Thus, again, the famous scene in which a lady is bandaging the foot of a gouty cavalier is said to be Augustus the Strong and the Countess Orselska. But most of these agreeable legends *are* legends. Until recently the two charming little figures in

FIG. 165. PASTORAL GROUP
By J. P. Melchior. Höchst; about 1770
Mannheim, L. Hunig Collection

Figs. 123 and 124 were called, by an ancient and sacred tradition, the Count and Countess Brühl. The most recent research has unkindly dispelled this illusion; the engravings from which both figures are modelled represent an English dandy and a London courtesan. Similarly the identification of a fine group, apparently Ludwigsburg, as Voltaire and Franziska von Hohenheim must now be queried, in spite of the strong resemblance of the cavalier to the French satirist.

Naturally all the Court factories produced portraits of the

ruling prince and members of his family, but they are almost always busts or reliefs, or modelled more or less in the monumental style of statuary. At a later date the princely factories began to produce pretty *genre* scenes, such as the one shown in Fig. 184, or the various handsome groups in late Vienna porcelain. Contemporary celebrities, generals, poets, musicians, and the like, were, of course, represented in busts

FIG. 166. CUPID AND A NYMPH
By J. P. Melchior. Höchst; about 1770
Frankfort-on-the-Main, Historisches Museum

and reliefs, especially during the last thirty years of the eighteenth century.

There is a further factor to be considered. Many groups which were formerly regarded as representations of fashionable society have turned out to be simply theatre groups. Knowledge of theatrical costume as prescribed by the French opera has shown the true significance of these figures; but of this I shall have something to say later.

Fashionable society was a theme which not a single factory cared to ignore; porcelain was essentially a luxury product, and porcelain plastic an art for the aristocracy. I need only

Goatherd and Shepherdess
By J. F. Lück. Frankenthal; about 1760
Munich, Bayerisches National-Museum

notice here the incomparable work of Bustelli. The illustrations will give various other examples of this art of kings.

Other classes too found a true portrait in the work of the porcelain-modellers. The merchant classes are strikingly portrayed in the Ludwigsburg shaving scene (Fig. 159), the Frankenthal groups *Concord in Marriage* (Fig. 150) and *Discord in Marriage* (Fig. 151)—the set being completed by a third group and entitled *Wooed, won, wed—The Dancing Lesson* (Fig. 143), and *The Good Mother* (Fig. 207). To these were added popular representations of other grades of society: artisans (Fig. 122), hawkers (Fig. 190), beggars, soldiers, musicians (Fig. 181), fishermen, gardeners (Fig. 174), miners (Fig. 117), and wood-cutters. There is scarcely a class or a trade which would not have found its own likeness in porcelain. 'Criers,' or street hawkers, occur very frequently both in series and as separate figures. Meissen and Vienna (Fig. 173), Berlin and Niderviller, produced lively little models of these characters of city life as we find them in the well-known *Cris de Paris*, or in a similar set of engravings appertaining to Vienna. From the beginning the comic quack was a godsend to porcelain-modellers (Fig. 125). Of course, there was a peasant to be fooled by him. But the peasant was rarely portrayed as a serious representative of the agricultural classes. Usually the scenes and figures of peasants are an odd mixture of the comic and dramatic, and quite obviously derive from Teniers and Brueghel. But it should be remembered that many of the peasant figures were not meant to be taken for life; peasants were simply the origin of fancy costumes worn at Society masquerades. This brings me to a section dealing with what was probably the most frequent stimulus in the invention of porcelain figures: I mean the diversions of Courts and the amusements of fashionable society—the masquerade, the opera, the stage, the ballet, and the chase.

(D) *Masquerades*

We are apt to think to-day that such amusements were the chief occupation of the Court and the aristocracy of those days, and, in fact, when we turn over the pages of contemporary memoirs it would seem that at many Courts, in Germany especially in Saxony and Württemberg, such things were cares of State. Enormous sums of money were spent on theatrical performances and masquerades. It is easy to realize how lavish such expenditure was when we read that the

FIG. 167. HUNTING FIGURES
By J. P. Melchior. Höchst; about 1770. See p. 275.
Formerly in the Mühsam Collection, Berlin

dancer Vestris received a half-yearly salary of 12,000 gulden from the Duke of Württemberg, that at Dresden the staging of a ballet often cost as much as 36,000 thalers, and that one of the industrial pageants (*Wirtschaften*) held at the Vienna Court involved an outlay of 3000 by each guest and his partner. These entertainments might be either professional plays or various kinds of amateur production. The latter, where the guests took part themselves, were much the more amusing. At the Court of the Dukes of Württemberg we learn that in carnival time there were two performances of opera and two masquerades each week. State officials, with their wives and daughters, were obliged to attend the masquerades, which were usually rather wild, unless they preferred to pay a heavy fine in the form of a deduction from their salaries. Masquerades of this kind were not limited to carnival time, but were

FIG. 168. BOY AND GIRL
By J. P. Melchior. Höchst; about 1770
Frankfort-on-the-Main, Historisches Museum

held at all seasons. There were several varieties of these mummeries: the masked ball proper, probably much the same as that of to-day, where every guest chooses his own fancy dress, or the fairs (*Jahrmärkte*), or industrial pageants, where there was a definite theme and where peasant costume was usually required. The guests were especially delighted if the edict went forth that the gentlemen were to appear as ladies and the ladies as gentlemen. Such a 'fair' was held as early as 1700 at Charlottenburg, and in 1719 we hear of a rustic wedding being celebrated in the palace at Vienna. Again, in 1768 a Venetian fair was introduced as the latest novelty by Charles Eugene, Duke of Württemberg, after his return from Venice. It was held in the market-place at Ludwigsburg, and Justinus Kerner remarks on it:

FIG. 169. GIRL FEEDING THE CHICKENS
By J. P. Melchior. Höchst; about 1770
Frankfort-on-the-Main, Historisches Museum

> The great market-place was covered with a big marquee, and buyers and sellers wore masks. There was a gaily coloured medley of masks taking part in the maddest games and processions, not the most striking among them being a monstrous jest of the Duke, who wore a baby's mask and costume and was carried round in a cradle and fed from a bottle by his nurse, who was a dwarf. From the windows of the administrative offices one got an excellent view of the market-place, and on such occasions the Duke took up his position there with his wife Franziska.

At a rustic wedding celebrated in the palace at Vienna, where the first industrial pageant had been held as early as 1573, the Emperor and Empress themselves played host and hostess. There also appeared a waiter, a cook, a chambermaid, a country lass, a minstrel, a quack, a schoolmaster, a captain, soldiers, village Jews, and peasants and peasant women of various European nations.

Most of the porcelain factories were in close contact with their respective Courts, and it is not surprising to find that all these masquerades are echoed in porcelain figures. Of the illustrations to the present work I need only refer to the pair of dancing peasants who seem to be taking off their masks (Fig. 155), and the Ludwigsburg booths at a fair (Figs. 161 and 162). The latter, with the charming little figures which

FIG. 170. LARGE SATIRICAL GROUP
By J. P. Melchior. Höchst; about 1775
Private possession

R

make up the set, are an epitome of the Duke's Venetian fair, although most of them were, in fact, produced before the first of these fairs was held.

Closely connected with the masquerade were pastoral plays. These were extremely popular as an amusement of fashionable society. It was great fun to assume the mask and costume of unsophisticated peasants, and play real games in a mood of frivolity and flirtation. Shepherd groups and figures were produced by all factories, and often carry a bird and open bird-cage as a symbol of love (Figs. 126 and 127). The largest and finest series of pastoral subjects was produced at Höchst by Melchior and his colleagues, but here we find sentimental naturalism and a romantic feeling for the simple unsophisticated life of rustic folk, which were characteristic of the 1770's (Fig. 165).

FIG. 171. THE OLD COQUETTE
Höchst; about 1783. See p. 218.
Hamburg, Museum für Kunst und Gewerbe

(E) *The Stage and Music*

The theatre in all its forms had a great influence on porcelain plastic of the eighteenth century. We are beginning to realize today that many of the groups and figures regarded as ladies and cavaliers, or as mythological figures, are really derived from the theatre, the opera, or the ballet. The theatre was probably the most important of eighteenth-century 'diversions.' Enormous sums were spent on staging opera and ballet, and famous opera singers and dancers, both men and women, received then, as they receive now, salaries which might well be envied by a minister of State. The theatre, moreover, for the world of fashion was not yet 'the drama,' which it became in the hands of Lessing and the classicists, but in the strictest sense of the word presented a 'show' on the

FIG. 172. GIRL WITH BASKET
Vienna; about 1760
Frankfort-on-the-Main, Kunstgewerbemuseum

stage, and made its appeal primarily to the eye. At this period we must distinguish between two types of theatrical performance: the set pieces of the regular stage—tragedy, opera, ballet—and the *commedia dell' arte*. The Italian comedy has its roots in an ancient popular tradition. It was not limited by the need for a large stage and elaborate properties, but could be performed anywhere with the simplest scenery. It was thus a kind of 'turn' in which everything depended on a spirited impromptu, and on the quick sympathy and combination of the whole troop. It made exceptional demands on the intelligence and presence of mind of the actors, far exceeding what is required of an actor who is not creating his part as he goes along, but simply following his 'lines.' The quick wits of Italy, trained for centuries in a close tradition of family and troop, had brought this type of theatrical performance to the highest accomplishment. During the sixteenth century a set of conventional characters had been evolved, which were easily identified by their conventional costumes; but the identification of them to-day is rendered extremely difficult from the circumstance that their names were frequently changed, apparently according to the region of Italy to which the troop belonged, and for other reasons not easy to establish. The principal actor was, of course, the Harlequin (Arlecchino), with his easily recognizable costume of coloured patch-work and his close-cropped head. He is never missing, and has only this one name. Recent research has shown that his part was created in Paris about 1575. But Brighella, the Intriguer or Busybody, who is also of French extraction, frequently appears as Scapin, Mezzetino, Zanne, and under other names. His characteristics are his beard, his long trousers and short cloak; his costume is variously coloured, being sometimes striped, sometimes trimmed with green. The externals of Pantalone, the comic Old Man, are stereotyped quite definitely; he always has red trousers, red cap, and black cloak, and wears a mask with a pointed beard. Another characteristic figure is the Doctor (Dr Balvardo, Dr Balanzoni, and so on), the comic Professor, always clad in black, with a huge hat and the flowing gown of the scholar. Pulcinella, the Merry Fellow, sticks to broad white smock and wide trousers; round his neck he wears a kind of ruff, and on his head a tall pointed hat. Like his German brother

(Hanswurst), he often has an enormous belly and a hump. The braggart, barnstorming Captain (Capitano Spavento, or Spezzamonti, etc.) is usually attired as a soldier; a nose of phenomenal size, huge moustaches, and a big sword at his side complete his martial equipment. The last male type is Pierrot, the Simple Servant (Pedrolino, Giglio, Bertoldo, Pagliacco), who wears a white mask over his white painted face, a white hat on his head, and a white costume with large buttons.

FIG. 173. FISH-SELLER
Vienna; about 1770
Frankfort-on-the-Main, Kunstgewerbemuseum

But if there was great variety of costume among the men it was even greater among the female parts. The *Amoureuse*, or *l'Accesa*, and the Serving-maid (*la Servetta*) went by very various names, not sanctioned by custom and tradition, but identical with the name of the actress who was playing the part, or determined by some other accident. The Isabellas, Silvias, Lelias, Ragondas, and Columbines all go back to the same female figures, which may be called collectively Columbine. It is important to note that there was no character costume for the women's parts; their feminine grace was in marked contrast with the grotesque attire of the men. Usually they wore the fashion of the day, or were dressed in a fanciful classical costume. The only exception was the female counterpart of the Harlequin, who likewise wore a costume of coloured patch-work. Similarly the women did not wear a full character mask, but, if masked at all, had only the black velvet domino of contemporary fashion, which had no distinguishing characteristics.

The great popularity of the *commedia dell' arte* is reflected in hundreds of porcelain figures. Scarcely a factory failed to produce at least a few 'comedy figures.' For the most part they were made in entire sets, as at Fürstenberg, Kloster-Veilsdorf, and Nymphenburg, where not only Harlequin and Harlequine, but no fewer than sixteen 'pantomime figures,' were modelled by the master hand of Bustelli. The earliest statuettes of this kind were made at Meissen in Böttger's red stoneware, and include some figures of splendid power, plastically conceived in the full baroque style (Fig. 104). *The Curious Harlequin* of Fig. 114 is a good sound, sensual piece of work, and illustrates the mature style of Kändler. Of the work of Bustelli, already mentioned, I illustrate three examples: Pantalone, with a lady who is here called Julia (Fig. 133), and the charming figure known as Leda (Fig. 132), though the lady's real name is uncertain. The two Fürstenberg figures of Columbine and Pierrot are much stiffer in treatment (Fig. 179). On the other hand, the Buen Retiro model in Fig. 199 is all Latin temperament and the wild rhythm of the South. The persons represented are certainly Harlequin and Pulcinella, while the figure standing behind may be the Doctor.

Many of the porcelain-modellers must have witnessed performances of Italian comedy, and were so taken with them that they copied them in porcelain. Many others took their figures from engravings. The latter are known from a set of twelve copper-plates with theatrical subjects engraved by J. B. Probst after designs by Schübler, and published at Augsburg in 1729; or, again, from seventeen plates by Joullain which illustrate Riccoboni's *Histoire du théâtre italien* (Paris, 1730). Copies of these designs are known to have been made at Meissen, and the figures in the Augsburg theatre designs were copied fairly closely by a modeller at Kloster-Veilsdorf. Bustelli's Pantalone is certainly derived from an engraving by

FIG. 174. GARDENING GIRL
Vienna; about 1770
Formerly in the Mühsam Collection, Berlin

Callot published as early as 1619. The painting of the figures sometimes varies, and departs from the comedy tradition, but

FIG. 175. BAGPIPER WITH PUPPET FIGURES
Vienna; about 1770
Formerly in the Mühsam Collection, Berlin

on the whole the decorative treatment is true to the colouring of the originals, and bears witness that the Italian comedy, though national in character, was familiar to every one.

From the 1770's representations of comedy subjects become less frequent, until they disappear altogether. Their place

FIG. 176. CAVALIER BEHIND A CHAIR
Vienna; about 1770
Formerly in the Mühsam Collection, Berlin

was taken by the drama. Figures representing the French drama had quite a different look from those of the extempore Italian comedies. In the first half of the eighteenth century the subject-matter of heroic drama was mainly derived from classical and mythological sources. Similarly, opera, which

FIG. 177. LADY SITTING TO A PORTRAIT-PAINTER
Group with cold painting. By A. Grassi
Vienna; about 1780
Frankfort-on-the-Main, Kunstgewerbemuseum

in the matter of costume usually followed the drama proper, took its themes mainly from classical antiquity and from the great heroic romances. At the present day the history of costume is so well known that it is not a little odd to find classical heroes appearing on the eighteenth-century stage in lace-boots, waistcoats of coloured silks with lace cuffs, short coats, and helmets with enormous plumes over large wigs. The Armidas, Iphigenias, and Dianas wore huge crinolines with rich embroidery and tightly laced bodices—in fact, followed contemporary fashions exactly like the ladies of the Italian comedy. The same thing applies to nymphs, shepherdesses, and gardening ladies, the differentiation of characters being effected entirely by their attributes, symbols, and style of ornament. The ballet, an essential part of opera and comedy, was similarly dressed; until about 1770 the male ballet-dancer (but not his partner) wore a mask. The social comedies of Molière and other writers were, of course, played entirely in contemporary costume. Historical realism in costume was first introduced in 1730 by Gottsched, but it made slow progress, and it was never brought to perfection; the 'old German costume' which came in during the last quarter of the eighteenth century, and was certainly regarded as 'real,' was simply the old Spanish costume with certain changes.

FIG. 178. STREET SINGER
Vienna; 1839
Vienna, S. Glückselig Collection

In recent years considerable numbers of porcelain figures have been identified as theatrical subjects, and not a few of Kändler's fine groups are ultimately derived from the drama or from opera. Among others Kändler modelled two charming groups of Count Rohan and the Marquise de Pompadour as Acis and Galatea, using for this purpose an engraving after a water-colour by C. N. Cochin. The latter reproduced a scene from an amateur performance given in the theatre at

Versailles in 1749. Fig. 115 shows a scene taken from a play, the actor in this case wearing Spanish costume.

Modellers in porcelain found frequent opportunities in the

FIG. 179. COLUMBINE AND PIERROT
Fürstenberg; about 1760. See p. 261.
Hamburg, Otto Blohm Collection

great productions of opera and ballet at the Courts of Charles Eugene of Württemberg and at the Mannheim theatre of Charles Theodore of the Palatinate. The magnificence of the settings, the enormous stage machinery, the lighting effects, and last but not least the dresses, which brought to

Ludwigsburg the leading costumier of the Paris opera and kept him busy for years—all this was a great drain on the finances of Württemberg. But it was also the pride and pleasure of his Highness; and we need feel no surprise that in

FIG. 180. PAIR OF DANCERS
By Desoches. Fürstenberg; 1771
Formerly in the Mühsam Collection, Berlin

1763 the great ducal factory was ordered to copy in porcelain an entire ballet which had been produced on the ducal birthday. The work was ready by the Duke's next birthday, and was in the form of a table centre-piece with elaborate figure ornament and the title *Le Bassin de Neptune*. Single dancers and groups of dancers are frequently found; the graceful group in Fig. 154 is an example, also of Ludwigsburg origin. The most famous *danseuses* of the day, Camargo and Sallé, were modelled by Frankenthal artists after French engravings, and two of the most beautiful Frankenthal figures, Oceanus and Thetis, are certainly derived from a ballet produced at Mannheim. Similarly the great Alcestis

FIG. 181. TWO MUSICIANS
Fürstenberg; about 1770
Formerly in the Mühsam Collection, Berlin

group originates quite certainly in the opera *Alceste*, which was produced there in 1775; the text, by Wieland, had been set to music by Schweitzer. A number of Sèvres groups also refer to various theatrical performances given by Marie-Antoinette in the theatre of the Petit Trianon. Towards the end of the eighteenth century the influence of the theatre on porcelain practically ceased. It may be noted, and it is not surprising, that we find no representation of the great dramas of Goethe and Schiller. Occasionally porcelain groups were suggested by one or other of the operas of sentimental uplift. Thus Fig. 130 shows the closing scene of Mme

Favart's opera *Annette et Lubin*, also taken from a contemporary engraving.

FIG. 182. SALT-CELLAR IN THE FORM OF A GIRL, ALLEGORICAL OF SPRING, GATHERING FLOWERS INTO A BASKET
Berlin; about 1765
Frankfort-on-the-Main, Kunstgewerbemuseum

Independently of grand opera and light opera, music itself has numerous echoes in porcelain. There are many groups representing music and musicians, from Kändler's beautiful

FIG. 183. FIGURE OF A CHINAMAN
By Friedrich Elias Meyer. Berlin; 1768
Berlin, Max Lang Collection

FIG. 184. FREDERICK THE GREAT AND PRINCE FREDERICK WILLIAM
By J. C. F. Riese. Berlin; about 1800. See p. 220.
Berlin, Max Lang Collection

spinet group (Fig. 112), Bustelli's *The Startled Sleeper* (Plate facing p. 210), and Beyer's famous *Musiksoli*, to the lively little Fürstenberg musicians of Fig. 181.

But music and porcelain are more fundamentally related; and the natural affinity between the music of Mozart and the

FIG. 185. CAVALIER AND LADY
Ansbach; about 1765
Mannheim, L. Hunig Collection

finest achievements in porcelain has been so aptly described by Max Sauerlandt that I cannot refrain from quoting his criticism in its entirety.

> Musical form in Mozart and plastic form in porcelain show the same lightness of touch and the same lively energy. In the line of a porcelain figure, as in the thread of a melody of Mozart, there is a pure and perfected grace. Each art has, too, the same ornament, rich and exuberant it may be, but never false to the inner and sustaining rhythm which informs the whole. Of tone, as of colour, there is the same gradation, the same prancing and dancing, of dazzling lights or vibrant sounds, the

same divine sanity of impulsive life. Both in Mozart and in porcelain the power of invention is almost uncanny. It starts from nothing, and it makes a world—a world where the human spirit, as it realizes and transcends its own nature, finds always new forms of self-expression, never failing in the freshness of their appeal, always touching our surprise, but never eluding our understanding. Each of these arts treads with a blind certainty in the narrow pathway of its own technique, but if we are quick to seize the intrinsic unity of a style which is common to both of them, I fancy that the fullest understanding of the music of Mozart will find itself somewhere enriched by the comparison; and the perpetual miracle which is the existence of Mozart will be a little nearer explanation if the creations of his musical fancy are writ small for us in the grace and gaiety of porcelain.

(F) *Hunting*

Hunting was almost the only sport of the eighteenth century. It amounted to a mania. No festival at Court ever passed without a hunt arranged in the most luxurious fashion and at enormous expense. The most fashionable form of hunting was *Parforcejagd* (a 'drive'), but this involved a practice which was essentially unsporting and ungentlemanly—that of driving the deer in procession past convenient shooting-butts, and then slaughtering them wholesale. Heron-hawking, with specially trained hawks, and partridge-shooting were favourite pursuits. Fashionable sports of this kind, in which Society ladies took an enthusiastic part, were naturally a good opportunity for the porcelain-modellers, and produced some fine groups and figures. Witness the Frankenthal *Mort Group* by J. W. Lanz (Fig. 140), the *Huntsmen from the Palatinate*, a charming group by K. G. Lück intended as a decoration for hunting banquets (Fig. 149), and the beautiful little figures representing duck-shooting (Fig. 167). The number of hunting subjects in porcelain is enormous. I have already remarked on them in discussing the painting of vessels. It is significant that they rarely come from Thuringia, although that country was thickly wooded and rich in deer. The Thuringian factories served a middle-class market, whereas hunting was the prerogative of courts and the aristocracy, who compelled the tenants on their estates to serve as beaters, and showed no little severity in enforcing their orders. Prints of the great sporting engraver Ridinger naturally had an influence on porcelain, especially at Nymphenburg, since the

FIG. 186. SHEPHERD AND SHEPHERDESS
Ansbach; about 1765
Mannheim, L. Hunig Collection

Court of Bavaria was as devoted to the chase as any in the whole of Germany.

(G) *Animals*

We find not only game, deer, and other quarry, but all sorts of wild beasts, reproduced in porcelain. For this, as for other subjects, the fashion was started by the great

FIG. 187. PAIR OF LOVERS
Ansbach; about 1765
Formerly in the Mühsam Collection, Berlin

Meissen modellers, Kirchner and Kändler, with the large animal figures ordered by Augustus the Strong for the adornment of the Japanese Palace. They are now an important part of the royal porcelain collection at Dresden, and make it look like a ceramic zoo. The *Specification of Porcelain required in the Royal Dutch Palace for the New Front Gallery*, which was sent to the management of the Meissen factory from Warsaw on

FIG. 188. FIGURES REPRESENTING WINTER (LEFT AND RIGHT) AND AUTUMN (CENTRE)
Fulda; about 1770–75. See pp. 288–289.
Frankfort-on-the-Main, A. Beckhardt Collection

April 2, 1732, enumerates no less than 214 "animals of all kinds, large and small," and 218 "birds of all kinds in various sizes," most of which were completed and delivered. These figures include every kind of creature, from the eagle and the cassowary to the coot, from the elephant and the rhinoceros to the jerboa—a complete fauna, both German and foreign. The originals of all animals not native to Germany were at the disposal of modellers in Dresden itself. A great princely household like that of Augustus the Strong, which set the example to the rest of Germany, possessed a pheasantry, a fish-garden, and a menagerie. The latter was housed in the hunting quarters at Dresden-Neustadt, where the 'beast-baiting' took place. A contemporary account says: "The menagerie gardens are so laid out that all the doors of the wild beasts' cages face the same way." The animals hunted included lions and tigers and other savage beasts, as well as stags, does, and wild boar. We know that the originals of some of the most beautiful animal figures modelled by Kändler

FIG. 189. THREE FIGURES
Fulda; about 1770–75
Mannheim, Hermannsdorf Collection

were on view in Dresden at the time. Such were Lithuanian aurochs, or bison, lions, tigers, lynxes, and a pelican, which seems to have been a very rare bird at that date; it was called *Löffel-gans*, or spoon-goose. The modeller lacked his original only in the case of the elephant and the rhinoceros, but he got some help from machines which had been made for Court *fêtes* and had been used for roundabouts as early as 1709 and 1714.

How Kirchner and Kändler used their opportunities for animal-modelling has already been discussed in connexion with the magnificently baroque Paduan cock shown in Fig.

110. The number of singing birds is legion, and at a later date they were made by nearly all factories. Parrots were great favourites, their fine gay plumage being a decorative opportunity. Of the animals the most popular were monkeys; then as now they always evoked the liveliest interest. They

FIG. 190. CLOTH MERCHANT
Kelsterbach; about 1765
Mannheim, Hermannsdorf Collection

were sometimes modelled in human dress, as is proved by Kändler's famous *Apes' Chapel*.

(H) *Mythology*

I have already pointed out, in discussing the theatre, the great importance of mythology in the cultural life of the eighteenth century. The humanist tradition was still a living thing. Scholars still spoke fluent Latin; Virgil and Ovid were real forces. The classical legends of gods and heroes were as familiar to men of middle class, whether lettered or merely educated, as they were to princes and noblemen. All of them in their youth had made the grand tour to France and Italy, and most of them had studied in one of the great Italian universities. The Court poet of the seventeenth and eighteenth centuries took care to keep a running comparison of his royal master with Mars, the god of war; his queen was Juno and his mistress Venus. The entire gallery of gods and heroes—Ovidian characters, as they were called—was as familiar to the general run of contemporary society as to sixth-form boys of to-day. Even porcelain-modellers were fairly well up in classical mythology. Of course, it is only in a few cases that we can assume first-hand knowledge of the classical poets; most of the modellers had not enough education to read for themselves. But they acquired considerable knowledge of the subject from engravings, and probably they obtained learned advice on mythology. Kändler, for example, is known to have been a man of education, and in his youth had studied the classical authors to some advantage, but, "as he now held his important post at Meissen, for several years he received daily lessons in the interpretation of the more difficult classical poets from Herr M. Weissen, who was then third master at the Royal School at Meissen."

FIG. 191. FIGURE OF A GIRL
Pfalz-Zweibrücken; about 1770
Mannheim, Hermannsdorf Collection

Mythology, in fact, took a very important place in the work of Meissen, as indeed of all the other porcelain factories. Gods and heroes, nymphs and tritons, the nine Muses, and a host of cupids, or *amoretti* (with wings) and *putti* (without wings), appear in single figures, or more usually in pairs or complete sets. It is characteristic of some factories—Nymphenburg, for example—that the gods themselves are replaced by charming *putti* with the attributes of the gods they stand for. Instances of mythological subjects here illustrated are two

FIG. 192. A BAGPIPER, REPRESENTING AUTUMN
Würzburg (?); about 1775. See pp. 287–288.
Frankfort-on-the-Main, A. Beckhardt Collection

Frankenthal groups modelled by Konrad Linck: *Meleager and Atalanta* (Fig. 145) and *Boreas and Oreithyia* (Fig. 144). One of Kändler's largest mythological groups is *Mount Parnassus*, with Apollo and Pegasus and the nine Muses all assembled (Fig. 202).

Clearly Mounts Olympus and Parnassus had to be brought in if it was intended to honour the royal house with a porcelain group depicting its apotheosis, as in Konrad Linck's group with the title *Vota Palatinatus exaudita* (Fig. 147). In 1774 Charles Theodore was stricken with a dangerous illness, and when he recovered his factory made this group for him, or possibly for some other client. Its rather ponderous allegory is

FIG. 193. THE LEMON-SELLER
Niderviller; about 1770
Formerly in the Mühsam Collection, Berlin

steeped in classical myth. On the right is the Lady Palatinate, with the armorial Palatinate lion crouching behind her, imploring the aid of the gods before the blazing sacrifice. The grief of the arts for their sick Mæcenas is personified by a weeping *putto*, who is bowed with sorrow over a palette and marble bust. But the gods have already done their duty: Pallas Athene leads down from Olympus her divine cousin

Hygieia, who treads beneath her feet the serpent of disease; and in front of her a second *putto* joyfully unveils the covered portrait of the sick monarch. On the altar shines the grateful

FIG. 194. FIGURES REPRESENTING EUROPE AND ASIA
Limbach; about 1775
Formerly in the Mühsam Collection, Berlin

legend *Vota Palatinatus exaudita.* These intricate allegories are numerous.

As the eighteenth century nears its end more modern heroes find a place among those of classical antiquity. In particular, from about 1760 Ariosto and Tasso were read considerably, and Rinaldo and Armida, and also Amynthas

Four Busts Allegorical of the Seasons

By K. Linck. Frankenthal; about 1765

Munich, Bayerisches National-Museum

and Sylvia, the hero and heroine of Tasso's pastoral play *Aminta*, begin to appear frequently in porcelain. A beautifully composed Höchst group of the latter is perhaps the most

FIG. 195. LADY AND GENTLEMAN WITH MUFFS REPRESENTING WINTER
Limbach; about 1780
Leipzig, Landesmuseum

charming of these Italian pieces, and has all the elegance and refinement of the early classical style.

(I) *Allegory*

Allegory is the expression of abstract ideas in anthropomorphic terms. It is an important factor in all artistic creations, and this is especially true of plastic or sculptural art. Allegorical personifications belong primarily to the age of baroque and rococo. Lessing in his *Laokoon*, published in 1766, sought to show that allegory is essentially inartistic, but the classical revival itself did not succeed in getting rid of it. On the contrary, allegory has persisted without inter-

FIG. 196. FIGURE OF A CAVALIER
Gera or Kloster-Veilsdorf; about 1780
Mannheim, Hermannsdorf Collection

ruption until the present day, and probably it will never quite disappear.

In the seventeenth century the Swiss covered the tiles of Winterthur stoves with illustrations of Bible stories; and in the worldlier *salons* of the eighteenth century chimney-pieces and wall-brackets supported porcelain figures, not only the gods of antiquity, but groups of the four elements, the four seasons of the year, and the four quarters of the globe. Any idea capable of personification, the cardinal virtues, the five senses, the seven liberal arts, the twelve months, the ages of

FIG. 197. FIGURES ALLEGORICAL OF SMELL AND HEARING
Zürich; about 1770
Hamburg, Otto Blohm Collection

man, time and eternity, war and peace, victory and renown—all these were modelled in endless sets, groups, and single figures, and attired in the impersonal drapery of classical antiquity, or more frequently in the costumes of contemporary fashion. All of which makes it sometimes very difficult to identify the idea represented by a particular figure.

It is difficult to see an allegory of autumn in the small bag-piper of Fig. 192, for which a Würzburg origin has been suggested, though not yet definitely proved. At the piper's feet there is certainly a basket of grapes, but the connexion is

FIG. 198. SULTANA AND EUNUCH
Copenhagen; about 1775
Hamburg, Museum für Kunst und Gewerbe

not clear until we have the other members of the set of the four seasons. The same thing applies to the charming little Fulda figures of a lady with a muff (Fig. 188). The fact that they signify winter does not make them any more beautiful, but there is a certain satisfaction in discovering the other members of the quartet. Again, in two Zürich figures representing two of the five senses (Fig. 197) the personification is fairly obvious. On the other hand, one cannot tell at a glance that the two

FIG. 199. CHARACTERS OF THE ITALIAN COMEDY PLAYING CARDS
Buen Retiro; about 1770. See p. 262.
Hamburg, Otto Blohm Collection

Limbach figures of royalties represent Europe and Asia (Fig. 194). A favourite practice was to represent each season by a pair of figures, as in the delightful lady and gentleman with muffs, which also come from the Thuringian factory of Limbach (Fig. 195). The pair of figures with the capital of a classical column and an architect's plan represent, of course, architecture (Fig. 152). Some of the prettiest allegories rendered in porcelain are Konrad Linck's figures of the

FIG. 200. PART OF THE RIM OF A MIRROR IN THE SCHLOSS PAULOWSK

Modelled by Boizot and presented by Louis XVI to the Grand Duchess Maria Feodorovna. Sèvres; 1781

months and seasons. He also modelled the latter in the form of small busts, as in the set shown in the Plate facing p. 284.

FIG. 201. GROUP IN BISCUIT PORCELAIN KNOWN AS "LES TROIS CONTENTS"
Modelled by Falconet after Boucher. Sèvres; about 1765
Munich, Bayerisches National-Museum

Erotic subjects, however, were the great stimulus to the inventive power of the porcelain-modeller. The thousands of love groups produced in all European factories have great charm, and are perhaps the truest memorial of the age of gallantry.

CHAPTER V

TABLE DECORATIONS AND ALTAR SETS

1. Table Decorations

THE æsthetic appeal of a work of art sometimes leads one to isolate it from its cultural background. This is an abstraction, since its cultural origin is the most important clue to its peculiarity of form. Decorative art, or 'applied' art, as it used to be called, has this advantage over 'fine' art, that with few exceptions it comes into existence to serve some definite purpose of man. Decorative treatment marks a certain refinement in objects of common necessity and common use. The bare essentials of serviceable form are dictated partly by custom and use, partly by the active endeavour of an age or a people to reduce the inconvenience of its own life. That fact explains, for instance, the evolution of form in furniture, from chests with a number of small doors to chests with large double doors, from the small upright chair to the more spacious armchair, and the diversity of types of furniture in the North and South of Europe. It explains, again, the difference between the graceful hemispherical bowl of a Venetian drinking-glass, made for a people who drank fine wine, and drank it with discretion, and the huge *Humpen*, from which the German toper preferred to consume beer. Finally, it accounts for the tiled stove of cold Northern climates and the fireplace of warmer countries.

Every form is determined by special conditions and serves a special purpose. To this general rule applied art provides a few exceptions, mainly in the field of ceramics. Most Italian maiolica dishes were not made with a utilitarian intention, but as decorations or show pieces for walls and sideboards. Similarly most vases of faience and porcelain made during the seventeenth and eighteenth centuries were designed as ornaments for walls, chimney-pieces, or furniture. In such cases the object is an end in itself, and in virtue of this in-

FIG. 202. "MOUNT PARNASSUS," WITH APOLLO AND THE MUSES

By J. J. Kändler. Meissen; about 1750–60. See p. 296.

Frankfort-on-the-Main, Kunstgewerbemuseum

dependence of purpose it is more or less on the same level as fine art. This criterion is applicable in a measure to porcelain figures. At the present day the whole art of modelling in porcelain is, of course, independent of any extraneous purpose, and its works are in the fullest sense fine art, just as the sister art of bronze figures is fine art. The same thing is true for the great majority of eighteenth-century porcelain figures, but in many instances—and they include some of the most important works in porcelain plastic—investigation has proved the exact contrary. Certain figures fulfilled a definite function in the decorative schemes of the period.

At all periods the decoration of the table has had a recognized place in the life of civilized peoples. From the fifteenth century onwards we can trace the custom of adorning the table with figure decorations in an architectural or landscape setting. At great festivals, royal weddings, or peace celebrations ornaments of various kinds, known in Germany as *Schaussen*, were arranged on the banqueting-table, and usually followed out some single theme. Mythological subjects were very popular. Often the entire classical pantheon must have made its appearance on the table, and the centre was then occupied by a representation of Mount Parnassus, surmounted by Apollo and Pegasus and the Muses. At wedding banquets the centre-piece was a Temple of Love surrounded by figures of the arts and virtues, which were to accompany the happy pair on their journey through life. Sometimes, again, the middle of the table revealed a strange world of 'Chinamen,' or an entire park, complete with arcades, grottoes, pools, trellis-work, garden statues, and animals, the latter freely copied from the heraldic beasts in the king's or prince's coat of arms. These *Schaussen* and table-centres were made of various materials, but the favourite substances were wax, tragacanth, and especially confectionery. Learned professors were often entrusted with the task of drawing up the subjects and scheme of the decoration, and it was carried out by a confectioner who had special experience in this class of work. But figures of wax or confectionery are ephemeral things, and after the invention of porcelain that material, being rich and delicate and well

FIG. 203. LARGE CENTRE-PIECE
By J. J. Kändler. Meissen; about 1755. See pp. 296–297.
Frankfort-on-the-Main, Kunstgewerbemuseum

suited for modelling, was at once applied to the making of table ornaments. This practice became so general that large numbers of the porcelain figures surviving to-day can be shown to have been made for table decoration. If this purpose is borne in mind it is at once evident that many groups were originally constituent parts of a great porcelain *ensemble*, and helped to carry out the idea embodied in it. The great pains taken by modellers to make their composition effective from any angle of approach are explained by the fact that their groups stood in the middle of the table, and must therefore be an artistic whole, equally agreeable from the point of view of any guest at the table.

The abundance of porcelain figures used for table decoration is revealed in an inventory, drawn up in 1753, of the confectioner's establishment belonging to Count Brühl, the great Saxon Minister and Commissioner for the Meissen porcelain factory. This inventory enumerates nearly all the figures produced at Meissen up to that date and, in addition, large numbers of big compositions, architectural pieces, and the like. Among the latter are four churches, two temples, three Italian towers, fifty-one town houses, thirteen peasants' cottages, five barns, thirteen stables, twenty niches, forty-eight pyramids, six gondolas, three dovecotes, a mill—also rocks, grottoes, pools, "bowls for fountains," altars, pedestals, columns and capitals, cornices and vases, crowns and Electoral hats, shields, palm-trees, flower-pots, orange-tubs, and so on. Among the larger structures appears a Temple of Honour in 264 pieces with 74 figures, a representation of Mount Parnassus, and a waterfall copied from the Ostrauer Garden. The only surviving example of the Parnassus group, made of large numbers of separate pieces, is illustrated in Fig. 202. According to the records the Temple of Honour was made in various shapes and styles, but only one complete specimen now exists; it is the property of the Kunstgewerbe museum at Frankfort-on-the-Main, and appears in Fig. 203.

This temple is Kändler's work, and dates from the 1750's. In every detail it exhibits the characteristic rococo forms of the period. There are twenty-four columns entwined with vine-stems and supporting a system of flat arches. Above the arches rises an ornamental cupola composed of shallow volutes and surmounted by a pinnacle in the form of a vase. The structure is enriched with *putti*, bearing shields or representing the seasons. It is composed of 114 separate pieces, and for its further security the bases of the columns, the rings round the capitals, and the rim running round the cornices are made of gilt bronze. Inside the temple is a group painted in gay colours: Cupid and Psyche plighting their troth before an altar, with Juno and her peacock hovering in the clouds behind. It is this group that gives the structure its character as a temple of love. In the liveliness and easy grace of its design this piece has all the spirit of rococo art, and its highly elaborate technique shows the limit of what the eighteenth century could achieve in the treatment of so delicate a medium as porcelain. If we remember the great technical difficulties involved in the perfection of smooth surfaces and sharp corners, and how in an architectural piece they are a necessary condition of success, we may pay a high tribute to the artistic merits of the design and to the technical accomplishment shown in the execution of it. The dimensions, moreover, are exceptionally large: height, $45\frac{5}{8}$ in., width, $33\frac{3}{4}$ in., depth, $23\frac{5}{8}$ in.

If we would form a correct impression of the effect which such a piece was intended to produce we should bear in mind that it was designed as the centre of a great banqueting-table, the peak and pivot of a decorative system. Marshalled all round it were its host of figures, vases, obelisks, and smaller architectural pieces, covering the whole table in orderly array, and laid out with the symmetry of a formal garden. The plates, bowls, dishes, and other vessels of the service completed the decorative whole, making a wonderful display of colour and a truly magnificent setting for a banquet. People the scene with the society for the delight of whose eyes it was created, cavaliers in their fine flowered suitings, ladies in patches and high powdered *coiffures* and dresses harmonious to the colours of the scheme, and you have rediscovered, as vividly and effectively as you may, the graces and gaieties of the age of rococo.

Fig. 204 gives a very clear idea of the style and arrangement of these table decorations. It reproduces the design for part of a large dessert service made by the Berlin factory in 1770-72 to the order of Frederick the Great as a present for 'his great enemy' the Empress Catherine II of Russia. The

FIG. 204. DESIGN FOR A SET OF TABLE DECORATIONS FOR THE EMPRESS CATHERINE OF RUSSIA
Berlin; 1770-72

centre-piece shows the Empress herself (modelled from a painting by Erichsen), seated beneath a canopy and surrounded by virtues and divinities. Round her throne are assembled four groups representing the classes of Russian society, while the table is dotted with single figures, embodying the various peoples of the Russian Empire; between them are trophies with captive Turks and groups allegorical of the liberal arts. The plates belonging to the service are painted in colours with scenes from the war with the Turks. The occasion of this honour in porcelain was political. Frederick the Great had made a defensive alliance with Russia, and in 1769, immediately after the outbreak of the first Russo-Turkish war, it was extended for a period of ten years. The great dessert service, modelled principally by W. C. Meyer,

FIG. 205. BANQUET AT THE WEDDING OF JOSEPH II AND ISABELLA OF PARMA AT VIENNA IN 1760

From a painting by Meytens in the Schönbrunn Palace

was one of the gifts exchanged by the two monarchs in token of their friendship. It is now in the Hermitage Museum at Leningrad.

Berlin produced several other large centre-pieces and accessories, but they are all late and characteristically of unpainted biscuit porcelain. Thus in 1793 a table set was designed by Hans Christian Genelli for the wedding of the Crown Prince Frederick William and Princess Luise of Mecklenburg-Strelitz. It was later extended by the addition of work by the modeller Riese, and in 1801 in this new form it went to Schwerin as a wedding present. The centre-piece consists of a group of Zephyrus and Psyche surrounded by geniuses and pairs of lovers. The two side-pieces are composed of girls carrying garlands and dancing round a raised copy of the antique group of Cupid and Psyche in the Capitoline Museum. A representation of Mount Olympus, of wide circumference and many figures, also goes back to a design by Genelli; it was completed in 1800, but only survives in fragmentary pieces. A dessert set, designed by Genelli as early as 1788, adorned the banqueting-table at the marriage of Princess Wilhelmina to the hereditary Stadtholder of the Netherlands (1791). A duplicate of this set, together with the dinner service belonging to it, consisting of hundreds of pieces, is preserved in the porcelain room at the Munich Residenz. Lastly, mention may be made of a great table set and dinner service presented to the Duke of Wellington in 1819 by Frederick William III. It cost 28,452 thalers; a number of river-gods, commemorating the Duke's victories, were modelled for it by Gottfried Schadow.

Similar sets with a single connected theme were certainly produced by the other German factories, and are known from various examples which survive. From the Vienna factory alone we have a whole series of such table decorations. Hunting sets were especial favourites; the most complete example of these is in the possession of Prince Auersperg at the castle of Slatina. It was made about 1750; and we may note in passing that the hunting group shown in Fig. 149 certainly belongs to one of these sets. At an earlier date a

Meissen set with curved balustrades, columns, and volutes had been copied at Vienna. But the largest work of the kind is a table set belonging to the monastery of Zwettl; it is more than four yards long and half a yard wide, and was made in the years 1767–68. A stand in nine pieces bordered with porcelain mouldings is covered with mirror glass, and on it stands a multitude of figures, mythological groups, *putti* groups personifying the arts, the four cardinal virtues, figures representing trades and classes, and numbers of *putti* in a variety of costumes. This set seems to have faced one way only, as does a similar set in a painting in the Schönbrunn Palace of the marriage of Joseph II and Isabella of Parma, which took place at Vienna in 1760 (Fig. 205). This picture shows the royal pair and a brilliant assembly of guests seated at a large table forming three sides of a rectangle; but the company sit only on the outside, the inside being left free for the service of waiters. Round the inner side of the table runs a long porcelain table set with white figures on a wavy stand. In front of the figures on the side nearest the diners are little bowls containing fruit or sweetmeats. These explain the term 'dessert,' which was applied to the Zwettl table set.

In 1797 Grassi had to design a table set for the wedding of the Archduchess Clementina to the Crown Prince of Naples. In doing so he introduced the famous sages and heroes of antiquity. This departure is characteristic of the new movement which came at the end of the eighteenth century. Things had been quite different a generation earlier. The great Ludwigsburg composition called *Le Bassin de Neptune*, which was set up in 1764 as a birthday present to Charles Eugene, Duke of Württemberg, shows a rocky waterfall with Neptune in his car surrounded by dolphins, tritons, naiads, *putti*, and fishes. It was an exact rendering in porcelain of a grand ballet which in the previous year had been magnificently produced in the ducal palace. Between these two table sets, both in time and in subject, comes a dessert service which was the prize in a lottery held in the town hall at Höchst in 1774. It included three "sleeping shepherd groups" and twelve "peasant children."

2. Altar Sets

From the point of view of pure decoration, which was expressed, as we have already seen, in the equipment of entire porcelain rooms, table sets were the only large systematic structures that the modellers in porcelain produced. On the same scale they turned out only one other type of porcelain outfit. This was the equipment for altars in churches. Augustus the Strong and his successor gave the Meissen factory two commissions of this kind, and these were the only large orders. The first was the complete equipment of the chapel in the Japanese Palace at Dresden, a big job and far from being an easy one. The order stayed on paper; the only parts of it actually carried out were the great statues of St Peter and St Paul modelled by Kändler and Kirchner (*cf.* Fig. 107), and several organ-pipes. The latter, with Kändler's St Peter, are now in the porcelain collection at Dresden.

Again, in 1737 Augustus III ordered a complete altar set, as a present for the Empress-Dowager Amelia. This was another big job, and was not yet complete in 1741 when the Empress-Dowager died. Eventually in 1750 it was sent to Vienna as a present for Maria Theresa, and there it still is, in the Kunsthistorisches Museum. It includes a crucifix, six altar candlesticks, a holy-water container, two Communion vessels, and statues of the Apostles modelled by Kändler from engravings of the baroque figures in St John Lateran at Rome.

Other large works by Kändler are a Crucifixion group, with numerous other figures, and the death of St Xavier. Smaller works include a *pietà*, the Madonna with St Anthony, and a figure of St Wenceslaus. The figure of St Nepomuk illustrated in Fig. 109 was modelled by Kirchner. Among the works of other factories are known to be Crucifixions, Madonnas, and various figures of saints intended for churches or for private devotions; and pretty holy-water basins are now of more frequent occurrence. In general, however, decoration in porcelain was foreign to the churches of the eighteenth century. Perhaps ecclesiastical feeling was afraid of the competition of loving couples and comedians and fools.

CHAPTER VI

SOURCES OF DESIGN IN PORCELAIN FIGURES

We have already shown to what extent engravings were used as models for paintings on vases and other porcelain vessels. Many groups and figures have a similar origin. But we may notice first that many of the finest modellers had creative ability and an entirely free hand. Kändler, Bustelli, Linck, Beyer, Melchior, and many others had no need of borrowed plumes. They were artists enough to design their own figures and groups; and their works remain the finest examples that we have of eighteenth-century plastic art. Yet few of them hesitated to make occasional use of the works of other artists, or even to copy them outright. Only in very few cases do we know, or can we even surmise, how far they were free agents in such matters, and how far they were merely obeying orders. Kändler, as we have seen, in modelling his Apostles for the altar set of the Empress Amelia had recourse to engravings of the baroque figures of the Apostles in the church of St John Lateran at Rome. We may perhaps suppose that he had a direct order to that effect from his royal client, more especially because free copies of the figures at Rome adorned the roof of the Hofkirch at Dresden, and were very popular in that city. On the other hand, it is scarcely surprising that a modeller as amazingly prolific as Kändler should be so taken with an outstanding work by another great master that he wished to adopt its figures and its composition as his own. It has been pointed out already that the charming lady in Fig. 111 is taken from an engraving, *Le Baiser rendu*, by Filloeul after Pater (Fig. 209). But the lady's partner, a cavalier in a dressing-gown, who is blowing her a kiss, may be regarded, till the contrary is proved, as Kändler's original work. Again, the beautiful lady spinning in Fig. 118 is known to be copied from a figure in a series of engravings by Surugue after

FIG. 206. LA BONNE MÈRE

Engraving by L. Cars after J. B. Greuze. See Fig. 207 and pp. 307–308.

Chardin, entitled *Les Amusements de la Vie privée*; the originals of the pair of figures known erroneously as Count and

Countess Brühl have already been identified. The more a modeller was lacking in originality the more dependent he would be on finding suitable models. The next step was to get hold of existing figures made in some other factory and modelled by a more talented artist. This was a frequent practice; the eighteenth century had no ideas of an artist's rights in his own work, still less of any legal protection; and it is an undoubted fact that original works were copied with no sort of check, and that originality in consequence became rather thin.

It is equally certain that the models copied at once enjoyed the greatest vogue with the general public. Fürstenberg copied a whole series of Meissen models, including a gardener and lady gardener, a shepherd and shepherdess, a man and woman selling *galanteries*, a girl feeding chickens, a 'musical monkey,' and others—all works which were great favourites about the year 1770. A spirited group by Bustelli, *The Listener at the Well*, called "the Inquisitive Piece" in the factory records, is known in the reproductions of several other factories, among them Frankenthal and Kelsterbach; and the Nymphenburg modeller Auliczek did not hesitate to make an almost exact copy of the Meissen perfume-burner illustrated in Fig. 129. Between Frankenthal and Höchst, Höchst and Fürstenberg, Fürstenberg and Berlin, Berlin and Meissen, Meissen and Vienna, Vienna and Capodimonte there is a long chain of imitation; besides which many modellers worked for several factories, and had a porcelain 'family' in two different places. Porcelain figures are an almost inexhaustible field, and the course of influence and imitation can be established only by special research into the work of particular factories. Decorative sculpture on a large scale, ivory figures, and bronze figures—all made occasional contributions to the design of porcelain, but original engravings and engravings of paintings were the sources of design most frequently used, both in the painting room and in the modelling room. It has been noted already that engravings were kept for this purpose by every factory.

It would be a great mistake to fall out with the modellers

on that account, or write down their efforts as hack-work. Servile imitations are, in fact, rare. In all these borrowings there is a high proportion of original work, and they all show unmistakably the idiom of their artist. We must remember,

FIG. 207. THE GOOD MOTHER
By K. G. Lück. Frankenthal; about 1770. See Fig. 206 and pp. 307–308.
Mannheim, C. Baer Collection

too, that the constant finding of new ideas and new subjects was far more difficult for the modellers of remote factories like Fulda, Ansbach, Fürstenberg, and most of the Thuringian undertakings than it was for their more favoured rivals, who worked in large cities and in the atmosphere of Courts, where every one was spiritually alive and interested in the arts. It is thus all the more remarkable that the modellers of a factory like Fulda should produce works of individual character and exceptional artistic merit.

It required considerable ability in a modeller to de-compose an engraved design in two dimensions and recompose it in the

FIG. 208. LE BAISER RENDU
Höchst; about 1755. See p. 308.
Frankfort-on-the-Main, Historisches Museum

round as a figure or group. It was not simply a matter of transcription, as it was for the painter on porcelain. This is evident in *The Good Mother* (Fig. 207), a Frankenthal group modelled by K. G. Lück after an engraving by Laurent Cars of a painting by J. B. Greuze (Fig. 206). The young mother with her baby is fairly close to the original; but there is a slight change in the position of the big boy, and the second child, asleep in a little chair, is turned right round, and serves to make the back of the porcelain group more interesting. But from the front as well this rounds off the group and improves the composition of the figures. The painter had a freer hand, since his background was filled in with the table and the cradle. Finally, Lück has the credit for a piece of common sense. The basket in the foreground is obviously too small to hold this well-developed infant, and Lück therefore substituted a proper cradle of suitable size by the side of the seated mother.

Figs. 208 and 209 provide another comparison. Here the porcelain-modeller is not half as good as the painter of the original subject, but he nevertheless acquits himself gracefully and cleverly. He had to deal with two contrasted engravings called respectively *Le Baiser donné* and *Le Baiser rendu*. In the first the nobleman is kissing the wife of a peasant. In the second the peasant gets his revenge and kisses the nobleman's wife, liking it so much that he exclaims:

> Ah, que ma joye auroit été complette
> Si Monsieur eut voulu coucher avec Lizette.[1]

This scene was, of course, designed in the flat, and it was not easy to recompose it in the round. The engraving, moreover, was explained by the accompanying verse, whereas the modeller had to make the situation clear simply by the position and expression of his figures. Thus he made the peasant a great lout of a fellow; the lady, who in the picture had smiled sweetly and treated the matter as a joke, is now a rather frightened woman, while the cavalier, who had watched the scene with an amused indulgence, has become an angry squire. The grouping of the figures is changed and simplified, and the accessories of the engraved version are omitted. The other engraving, *Le Baiser donné*, was similarly modified. What a greater artist could make of the same original subject may be seen in Fig. 111. There Kändler has isolated the graceful and charming lady of the engraving and made one of his best crinoline figures, giving her for a partner an exquisite young man who blows her kisses. Equally sensitive

[1] How great had been my happiness
If Squire had gone to bed with Bess.

FIG. 209. LE BAISER RENDU
Engraving by Filloeul after Pater. See Fig. 208 and p. 308.

is the treatment of hundreds of other groups—for example, the Höchst group already mentioned of Amynthas and Sylvia after Bouchardon, and *The Old Coquette* (Fig. 171), after an engraving by Göz entitled *Supplément des Graces effanées*. Other comparisons might easily be drawn, but I mention only works illustrated in this book and the engravings from which they are known to be derived. Thus the exquisite Meissen group of a Chinese lady and two children (Fig. 119) follows an engraving by J. J. Bachelier after Boucher's *Délices de l'Enfance*; and the pastoral music-lesson in the Plate facing p. 252 was modelled at Frankenthal from an engraving by R. Gaillard of Boucher's *L'Agréable Leçon*.

But whether porcelain figures are the original designs of their modellers or only copies of engravings, they are in any case things of beauty and the mirror of an age. They reveal the humanity of the eighteenth century in every phase of its social life, living and doing, dancing and being diverted, in full dress and undress, in its poses and its flirtations. Beauty was admired, and the arts flourished, endless in their diversity, alike in their elegance and power. Porcelain is an expression of the eighteenth century; that is its appeal to our own.

BIBLIOGRAPHICAL NOTE

The German edition of this book contains no bibliography, and much of the literature to which it alludes is German. Even a selection from the literature of porcelain would run into many pages, to say nothing of the historical background, relations between China and Europe, and the allied arts to which the author refers. What follows is only a brief list of the most interesting and important books which deal specifically with porcelain. It is intended primarily for English readers, and since most of the works cited themselves contain bibliographical material it should be sufficient to open up the literature of the subject. Owing to the necessity for illustrations many of the books are costly, the price being as often in guineas as in shillings. Some of them are scarce and only obtainable in libraries. The great advances made in the study of the history of porcelain during the present century make recent books the more valuable.

CHINESE PORCELAIN

The most valuable book in many ways is still:

BUSHELL, S. W.: *Oriental Ceramic Art* (New York, 1899).

This work represents an earlier stage in knowledge, but it contains a great body of technical and iconographical information, including translations from Chinese native sources, and has been extensively drawn upon by most later writers. There are no illustrations. Bushell wrote his text for a large work on an American collection:

BUSHELL, S. W.: *The W. T. Walters Collection* (New York, 1897).

The ten sections (volumes) of this work are superbly illustrated, but of such monstrous size as to be of little practical use.

The next landmark was:

HOBSON, R. L.: *Chinese Pottery and Porcelain* (2 vols., London, 1915).

Except for specialized study and for certain later discoveries, this contains all the information that is normally required; but it is now very costly. The following special studies are more accessible, and cover between them the whole of the later history of Chinese ceramics:

HOBSON, R. L.: *The Wares of the Ming Dynasty* (London, 1923).

HOBSON, R. L.: *The Later Ceramic Wares of China* (London, 1925).

A good book for the early history of Chinese porcelain until the Sung dynasty is:

HETHERINGTON, A. L.: *The Early Ceramic Wares of China* (London, 1923).

Most recent research is resumed in:

HOBSON, R. L.: *The Eumorfopoulos Collection. Catalogue of the Chinese and Japanese and Corean Pottery and Porcelain* (London, 1925–28).

This great catalogue, dealing with a world-famous collection, is in six volumes, of which the last three deal largely with porcelain. It is magnificently illustrated. More, perhaps, can be learned from it than from any other work, though not more easily.

There is no introduction to Chinese porcelain which is both cheap and good. The best substitute for one is to be found in the section dealing with pottery and porcelain in the second volume of:

BUSHELL, S. W.: *Chinese Art* (London, 1906).

But this book is pre-Hobson and not very interesting to read.

There are two good museum guides, both illustrated:

HOBSON, R. L.: *Guide to the Pottery and Porcelain of the Far East* (London, British Museum, 1924).

HONEY, W. B.: *Guide to the Later Chinese Porcelain: Periods of K'ang Hsi, Yung Chêng and Ch'ien Lung* (London, Victoria and Albert Museum, 1928).

CONTINENTAL PORCELAIN

The information in English books on Continental porcelain is largely second-hand. The best book is a translation from the Danish:

BIBLIOGRAPHICAL NOTE

HANNOVER, E.: *Pottery and Porcelain*. Translated from the Danish. Edited with supplementary notes by BERNARD RACKHAM (3 vols., London, 1925).

This is a 'monumental' work, of which the third (and last) volume deals with European porcelain, including English; but English porcelain is better studied elsewhere (see below). This book is very clearly arranged and easy to use, in spite of the great mass of information which it contains. It takes its subject by countries and factories, giving a short history of each factory, critical descriptions of its work, and illustrations of characteristic pieces, but no marks. The illustrations are numerous and drawn from public and private collections all over Europe. There is also a very full classified bibliography, with additions by the editor. On certain points Hannover has recently been called in question, but at the time of writing there is no other work of equal amplitude and authority. W. B. HONEY has in preparation an encyclopædia of ceramics which promises in some respects to supersede it. There is also in preparation a good book in German by F. H. HOFMANN.

GERMANY

The more important monographs are given below. Some of the minor factories have not yet acquired monographs. The literature about them is largely contained in periodicals; clues to it will be found in the bibliography of Hannover's work, mentioned above.

Berlin

LENZ, G.: *Berliner Porzellan: Die Manufaktur Friedrich des Grossen, 1763–86* (2 vols., Berlin, 1913).

Frankenthal

HOFMANN, F. H.: *Frankenthaler Porzellan* (2 vols., Munich, 1911).

HEUSER, E.: *Porzellan von Strasburg und Frankenthal* (Neustadt-an-der-Haardt, 1922).

Fürstenberg

SCHERER, C.: *Das Fürstenberger Porzellan* (Berlin, 1909).

Höchst

RÖDER, K., and OPPENHEIM, M.: *Das Höchster Porzellan auf der Jahrtausend-Ausstellung am Mainz, 1925* (Mainz, 1930).

A good catalogue, beautifully illustrated.

HOFMANN, F. H.: *Johann Peter Melchior* (Mainz, 1921).

Ludwigsburg

BALET, L.: *Ludwigsburger-Porzellan* (*Figurenplastik*) (Stuttgart, Leipzig, 1911).

CHRIST, H.: *Ludwigsburger Porzellanfiguren* (Stuttgart, Berlin, 1921),

Meissen (Dresden)

BERLING, K.: *Das Meissner Porzellan und seine Geschichte* (Leipzig. 1900).

BERLING, K.: *Festive Publication to commemorate the 200th Jubilee of the Oldest European China Factory, 1910* (Meissen, 1912).

This book is written in very strange English, but for readers who have no German it is a useful substitute for *Meissner Porzellan.*

Nymphenburg

HOFMANN, F. H.: *Geschichte der bayerishen Porzellan-Manufaktur Nymphenburg* (3 vols., Leipzig, 1921–23).

HOFMANN, F. H.: *Das Europäische Porzellan* (Munich, 1908).

This is a catalogue of the Nymphenburg porcelain in the Bayerisches National-Museum, at Munich, including the famous collection of figures by Bustelli; also useful for other European porcelain.

Thuringian Factories

GRAUL, R., and KURZWELLY, A.: *Altthüringer Porzellan* (Leipzig, 1909).

Vienna

FOLNESICS, J., and BRAUN, E. W.: *Geschichte der kaiserlichköniglichen Porzellan-Manufaktur* (Vienna, 1907).

Figures

FALKE, O. VON: *Deutsche Porzellanfiguren* (Berlin, 1919).

SAUERLANDT, M.: *Deutsche Porzellanfiguren des 18-Jahrhunderts* (Cologne, 1923).

FRANCE

CHAVAGNAC, X. DE, and GROLLIER: *Histoire des Manufactures françaises de la Porcelaine* (Paris, 1906).

The standard work on French porcelain.

LECHEVALLIER-CHEVIGNARD, G.: *La Manufacture de Porcelaine de Sèvres* (Paris, 1909).

The standard work on Sèvres.

BIBLIOGRAPHICAL NOTE

AUSCHER, E. S.: *A History and Description of French Porcelain.* Translated from the French by WILLIAM BURTON (London, 1905).

An introductory work, but published before either of the two books last mentioned.

For the other French factories reference may be made in the first instance to Hannover's bibliography.

ITALY, SPAIN, THE NETHERLANDS, SWITZERLAND, DENMARK, RUSSIA, AND OTHER CONTINENTAL COUNTRIES

The literature is largely in languages not generally familiar to English readers, and much of it is contained in periodicals. There is a classified list in Hannover.

ENGLISH PORCELAIN

The Victorian classic of the subject is:

JEWITT, L.: *Ceramic Art of Great Britain* (London, 1878).

This book is a great collection of information, original documents, lists of potters, and the like, but must now be used with circumspection. Modern study of English porcelain was created by two catalogues:

RACKHAM, B.: *Catalogue of the Schreiber Collection of English Porcelain, Earthenware, Enamels, etc.* Vol. I. *Porcelain* (second edition, London, Victoria and Albert Museum, 1928).

The second edition, not the first, is the book to read.

RACKHAM, B.: *Catalogue of the Herbert Allen Collection of English Porcelain* (second edition, London, Victoria and Albert Museum, 1923).

This book stresses the later wares.

Both these works are encyclopædic in range and profusely illustrated. The objects are catalogued by factories, each section being preceded by a brief history of the factory in question. Though more for study than perusal, the second edition of the catalogue of the Schreiber Collection in particular is easy to use, even for those who have no previous knowledge of the subject.

The best *general* account of English porcelain is:

Honey, W. B.: *Old English Porcelain* (London, 1928).

This may be regarded as a summary of the two catalogues mentioned, but contains much new matter and the most complete set of marks in existence. It is a handbook rather than an introductory summary.

Attributions of English porcelain to the various factories are partly based on chemical analysis of the body; for this see a *brochure* published by the Victoria and Albert Museum:

Eccles, H., and Rackham, B.: *Analysed Specimens of English Porcelain* (London, 1922).

A book by a potter is:

Burton, W.: *A General History of English Porcelain* (third edition, London, 1921).

A book by a chemist may also be recommended:

Church, Sir A. H.: *English Porcelain* (London, 1904).

But this, and a number of other works not noted here, is best described as pre-Rackham.

The *factory monographs* vary a good deal in value. In the list below the best are those marked with an asterisk.

Bow

Mew, E.: *Old Bow China* (London, 1909).
Hurlbutt, F.: *Bow Porcelain* (London, 1927).

Bristol

Hurlbutt, F.: *Bristol Porcelain* (London, 1928).

Chelsea

*King, W.: *Chelsea Porcelain* (London, 1922).

Derby

Haslem, J.: *The Old Derby China Factory* (London, 1876).
Hurlbutt, F.: *Old Derby Porcelain and its Artist Workmen* (London, 1925).

William Duesbury

*Macalister, Mrs D.: *William Duesbury's London Account Book.* Edited, with an introduction (London, English Porcelain Circle, 1931).

A valuable recent discovery.

Longton Hall

BEMBROSE, W.: *Longton Hall Porcelain* (London, 1906).

Lowestoft

SPELMAN, W. W. R.: *Lowestoft China* (London, Norwich, 1905).

Swansea and Nantgarw

TURNER, W.: *The Ceramics of Swansea and Nantgarw* (London, 1897).

Worcester

*HOBSON, R. L.: *Worcester Porcelain* (London, 1910).

*HOBSON, R. L.: *Catalogue of the Frank Lloyd Collection of Early Worcester Porcelain* (London, British Museum, 1923).

Figures

*KING, W.: *English Porcelain Figures of the Eighteenth Century* (London, 1925).

Toys (Chelsea)

*BRYANT, G. E.: *Chelsea Porcelain Toys* (London, 1925).

BOOKS OF MARKS (GENERAL)

The leading English encyclopædia of marks has been for many years:

CHAFFERS, W.: *Marks and Monograms on European and Oriental Pottery and Porcelain* (fourteenth edition, edited by H. M. CUNDALL, London, 1928).

This is more valuable for reference than for ordinary perusal.

The best general mark book, covering all varieties of porcelain (including Chinese), is:

BURTON, W., and HOBSON, R. L.: *Handbook of Marks on Pottery and Porcelain* (revised edition, London, 1928).

It is of convenient size and low price, and for general purposes exhaustive. For English porcelain it may be supplemented by HONEY's book (see above).

A useful book for the later English wares is:

RHEAD, G. W.: *British Pottery Marks* (London, 1910).

INDEX

Italic figures refer to the illustrations and their legends.

INDEX

INDEX

INDEX

INDEX

INDEX

NY SOCIETY LIBRARY 53 E 79ST NY NY 10021
3 0000 00007116 1